Canada
Japan
United States
inese Taipei
Mexico
Kong,
Philippines
salam
Papua
New Guinea
Peru
Chile
Australia
New Zealand

APEC AT 20

The **Institute of Southeast Asian Studies (ISEAS)** was established as an autonomous organization in 1968. It is a regional centre dedicated to the study of socio-political, security and economic trends and developments in Southeast Asia and its wider geostrategic and economic environment.

The Institute's research programmes are the Regional Economic Studies (RES, including ASEAN and APEC), Regional Strategic and Political Studies (RSPS), and Regional Social and Cultural Studies (RSCS).

ISEAS Publishing, an established academic press, has issued almost 2,000 books and journals. It is the largest scholarly publisher of research about Southeast Asia from within the region. ISEAS Publishing works with many other academic and trade publishers and distributors to disseminate important research and analyses from and about Southeast Asia to the rest of the world.

APEC AT 20

RECALL, REFLECT, REMAKE

edited by

K. KESAVAPANY

HANK LIM

ISEAS

INSTITUTE OF SOUTHEAST ASIAN STUDIES

Singapore

1. APEC Economic Leaders' Meeting, Bogor, Indonesia, 15 November 1994. The Bogor Goals provided a sharp focus to the vision of regional economic cooperation. *Photo courtesy of the APEC Secretariat.*

Contents

First published in Singapore in 2009 by ISEAS Publishing
Institute of Southeast Asian Studies
30 Heng Mui Keng Terrace
Pasir Panjang
Singapore 119614

E-mail: publish@iseas.edu.sg
Website: <http://bookshop.iseas.edu.sg>

ISEAS Library Cataloguing-in-Publication Data

APEC at 20 : recall, reflect, remake / edited by K. Kesavapany and Hank Lim.
1. Asia-Pacific Economic Cooperation (Organization).
2. Asian cooperation.
3. Pacific Area cooperation.
4. Asia—Economic policy.
5. Pacific Area—Economic policy.
I. Kesavapany, K.
II. Lim, Hank, 1939-
HF1583 A631 2009

ISBN 978-981-4279-26-0 (hard cover)
ISBN 978-981-4279-27-7 (E-book PDF)

Cover Photos:
APEC's beginnings when the first informal meeting of Ministers was held in November 1989 in Canberra, Australia, consisted then of only 12 member economies. The new APEC Secretariat Building in Singapore represents, in a way, the solid foundation for meeting the challenges and moving APEC ahead in this new millennium. APEC now has 21 member economies and includes most of the major developed and developing economies around the Asia Pacific. *Photos courtesy of the APEC Secretariat.*

Endpaper:
The map showing the 21 APEC member economies was kindly provided by the APEC Secretariat.

Typeset by Superskill Graphics Pte Ltd, Singapore
Printed in Singapore by Utopia Press Pte Ltd

Foreword

Twenty years is not a long time in the life of a regional process. I was involved with APEC at its conception and have returned. Observing the evolution of APEC in the intervening years has been akin to watching patiently the seemingly undirected behaviour of ants in a colony.

APEC in the late 80s was more a desire than a plan of action. You could perhaps detect it in the glint of the eyes of the founding fathers. Their desires were basic and instinctual — to create a process that would give form and shape to the Asia Pacific, to bring growth and prosperity to the region. Yet, arguments raged about the fundamentals of membership, substance and direction.

So, when APEC came into being in 1989, it was with just 12 members in a loose consultative forum, with no organizational structure, without a large bureaucracy supporting it, and with a limited programme of sectoral cooperation.

APEC took a sharp turn in1993 with the first Leaders' meeting in Seattle. By the following year, APEC had united the region's Leaders around the common goal of free and open trade and investment in the Asia Pacific. This was no mean feat considering the diversity and geo-political heft of its members.

Since then, APEC has grown in depth and scope. With close to 150 meetings, Leaders, officials and businesspeople meet throughout the year to debate and formulate new ways of advancing regional economic integration and to clear the paths for business to navigate across our borders.

Today, many critics still maintain that APEC is hampered by its own rules of consensus decision-making, that targets are aspirational rather than binding and that liberalization is at most unilateral.

I would dispute that summation because it fails to understand that APEC is a complex phenomenon, much like the World Wide Web which also celebrates its 20th anniversary this year. The WWW grew from a scientific project to a global phenomena that has reshaped the way the market works and touched the core of our lives.

In similar fashion, APEC has grown like an organism, achieving progress, not through legalistic formal mechanisms but through the disparate efforts of the clusters of people working in different sectors to advance regional well-being and growth. Think of APEC's innovations using the pathfinder approach to explore new ways of regional integration; building convergence through the sharing of best practices; bringing the business world into the soul of APEC activities.

Hence, the test of APEC in the next 20 years will not lie in its speeches or declarations but in its concrete responses to the challenges ahead and in the level of innovation and creativity it brings to bear on these issues. I look forward to writing the next Foreword in 2029.

Ambassador Michael Tay
APEC Executive Director

Preface

This year marks the 20th anniversary of the inaugural Ministerial-level meeting held in Canberra in November 1989, which officially launched Asia-Pacific Economic Cooperation (APEC). Publishing a commemorative book on APEC's first 20 years thus seems opportune. In particular, a significant contribution to the existing extensive literature on APEC would be a collection of essays by "old hands" on APEC. Hence, the chosen title for this commemorative book. "APEC at 20: Recall, Reflect, Remake" contains personal and candid recollections and reflections of academics and policy analysts who have a longstanding involvement in APEC on the background of APEC, how its agenda have evolved in the last twenty years, its successes and challenges, as well as their prognoses on its the future, including the need to remake APEC.

Andrew Elek covers the birth of APEC, its overall goals, objectives and guiding principles, the major milestones since its inception, the challenges it faces and its prospects. He rightly points out that the foundations for APEC were laid long before its official launch twenty years ago. He notes both its achievements and disappointments. And he argues that APEC's 20th anniversary can be an opportunity to recover credibility, as well as a time to reaffirm the concept of open regionalism.

Peter Drysdale likewise notes that the first step in considering how APEC might move forward in the future is to recall APEC's origins and the processes on which it is built. In particular, APEC's governing principle of open regionalism entailed a great deal of innovative thinking to come up with a new form of regionalism that would fit the circumstances of the Asia Pacific. Twenty years later, we see the emergence of the new regionalism in East Asia, and growing bilateralism and a move towards sub-regional FTAs that run counter to the principles upon which APEC was designed. A crucial issue for East Asia's global agenda then is to define a relationship between East Asian cooperation and integration that is complementary to trans-regional cooperation in Asia and the Pacific. But APEC's preeminence in the Asia Pacific region persists despite the complementary evolution of East Asian regionalism. The future of APEC depends on how the Asia Pacific region moves to resolve the question of the relationship between the development of economic and political cooperation in East Asia and trans-Pacific cooperation with newly-developing South Asia.

Charles Morrison's essay also argues that the true measure of APEC's significance will lie in whether it is widely perceived to have had a transformative impact on prospects for international order in the Asia-Pacific region and globally, and whether it leads to something more. His evaluates some of the limitations and obstacles APEC confronts and concludes with suggestions about how the architecture of Asia-Pacific cooperation might be enhanced. In particular, he cites three key areas that the current regional architecture, including APEC, needs to address: the coverage of regional security; the extent to which the region consults on global issues; and rapid responses to new challenges. He argues that finding national champions for the regional process is probably the most important requirement for a new wind of broad Asia-Pacific cooperation. Australia and Japan had played this role in the early years of APEC. In contrast, the United States has rarely played this role despite its obvious interests in the region. He hopes the new American leadership, combined with a set of changing international relations dynamics that encourage multilateralism in U.S. policy, proves to be the new wind in the sails of the noun "APEC" and trans-Pacific regional cooperation.

In her essay, Man-jung Mignonne Chan assesses APEC from three dimensions: participants, modality, and APEC as an institution in the geopolitical dynamics. She distinguishes between three types of APEC participants — liberal/idealists, realists, and constructivists, and their respective impacts on unilateralism, multilateralism, and constructivism. The nature of participants is core to the APEC process since it affects not only the project initiatives, stakeholders' participation eligibility and membership expansion, but also determines institutional identity, level of confidence, and future outlook of APEC. Chan then discusses APEC's chosen modality of concerted unilateralism, including its implementing framework consisting of CAPs, IAPs, and peer review process; the criticisms against it, as well as how to move it forward; and the alternative approach of competitive liberalization, including the FTAAP. Finally, on APEC as an institution in the geopolitical dynamics, Chan argues that APEC has provided numerous opportunities for people-to-people contacts that have fermented a strong sense of community, and promoted regional peace and prosperity.

Zhang Yunling and Shen Minghui track APEC's progress in terms of the three pillars of its work programme through a series of initiatives undertaken in the past two decades. Key challenges remain. First is how to realize its Bogor Goals. Another challenge to APEC is how to realize its commitment of reducing economic development gaps. A new challenge to APEC is how to reduce the negative effect of the "noodle bowl" (spaghetti bowl) caused by the multilayered bilateral and sub-regional FTAs/EPAs. Considering the great diversity of APEC members, they do not think it is realistic to expect that APEC could initiate an APEC wide FTA agenda based on negotiations in the near future. Instead, they argue that APEC should become more active and effective in dealing with the current financial crisis, reform of the international financial system, domestic reforms on both financial and economic structures, as well as the post crisis agenda like sustainable and balanced trade structure and relations in the Asia-Pacific region. And China will continue to have strong interest to participate in APEC activities and to support its playing a positive role in promoting regional economic integration and cooperation.

Hadi Soesastro's essay presents an in-depth analysis of APEC's Bogor Goals and the choice of modality to realize them, the challenges of implementation and its strengthening over the years, and finally the need for a revamp. He reviews why and how the Bogor Goals were crafted, which also explains the adoption of the concept of concerted unilateral liberalization to achieve those goals. He then examines how this concept was made operational, including key initiatives undertaken over the years to improve it, particularly the peer review process. Finally, he examines areas for considerations in strengthening the peer review process, which he deems a key element to revamping APEC's concerted unilateral liberalization.

Ippei Yamazawa's essay likewise looks at the Bogor Goals, particularly the Osaka Action Agenda and IAP/CAP framework. He discusses how the IAP/CAP framework tracks APEC's progress in trade and investment liberalization and facilitation, and economic and technical cooperation. He notes that the challenge for Japan, as APEC host economy in 2010, is how to graduate the developed member economies from their Bogor commitment. Like Zhang and Shen, one option that he identifies is to suspend the Bogor Goals. At the same time, all member economies should be encouraged to pursue the expanded Busan Roadmap. Ultimately, he suggests the graduation route as the agenda for APEC 2010. That is, graduate APEC's five developed economy members together with Singapore, Chile and Hong Kong, China; encourage the rest to remain engaged in the Bogor commitment; and set a post-Bogor agenda for the graduating group towards a higher level of liberalization and to complete the remaining agenda in the Busan Roadmap.

Finally, Tommy Koh, Lee Tsao Yuan and Arun Mahizhnan provide a succinct narration of the inception of the Pacific Business Forum, which served as precursor to the very influential APEC Business Advisory Council (ABAC). As they rightly pointed out, APEC Economic Leaders' unprecedented approach of directly and formally engaging the business community as part of the APEC deliberative process, initially through PBC and later through ABAC, has proven auspicious.

We would like to acknowledge all those who contributed to this book particularly Tommy Koh who first suggested publishing such a commemorative volume. First of all, we express our appreciation to the Organizing Committee of APEC Singapore 2009 for supporting this project. We are most grateful to the paper writers for agreeing to contribute to the book despite the very tight deadline that we gave them. We also thank the APEC Secretariat for giving us access to their archive of photographs and key information about the member economies of APEC.

We are pleased to release this book on the 20th anniversary of APEC. The book comes out at a time when the role and relevance of APEC, more than ever, is being reexamined, even questioned. But the essays in this book have indicated a continuing, albeit changing role for APEC regionally and globally, and have identified options on how to develop APEC and the APEC agenda to ensure its relevance in the years ahead. We hope this book will help readers to have a better understanding, and hence appreciation of APEC — what it truly stands for and what it aims to accomplish.

K. Kesavapany
Director
Institute of Southeast Asian Studies

Hank Lim
Director of Research
Singapore Institute of International Affairs

August 2009

About the Authors

The Editors

K. Kesavapany is Director of the Institute of Southeast Asian Studies (ISEAS) and Director of the Singapore APEC Studies Centre at ISEAS. Prior to 2002, Ambassador Kesavapany was Singapore's High Commissioner to Malaysia. In his 30-year career in the Foreign Service, he served as Permanent Representative to the United Nations in Geneva from December 1991 to March 1997, and has held key appointments in the Ministry of Foreign Affairs (MFA), Singapore. He was an active participant in the final phase of the Uruguay Round negotiations where he was elected the first Chairman of the WTO's General Council in 1995. He was also involved in the first APEC Senior Officials Meeting and the PECC process at the MFA, Singapore.

Hank Lim is currently Director for Research at the Singapore Institute of International Affairs (SIIA). Prior to joining SIIA, Dr Hank Lim was a faculty member at the Department of Economics, National University of Singapore. He has extensive experience and exposure in international and regional cooperation issues. His areas of specialization include ASEAN, APEC and East Asian economies. He was the first Singapore Representative to the APEC Eminent Persons Group (EPG). From 1990 to1993, he served as the first Director-General of the Pacific Economic Cooperation Council (PECC) International Secretariat in Singapore. Dr Lim has received numerous awards, including a Fulbright Fellowship and Japanese Ministry of Finance Foundation of Advanced Information Research (FAIR) award. He was appointed as an Expert for the APEC IAP Review of China in 2004 and of the Philippines in 2009.

The Contributors

Andrew Elek is Executive Director of Bellendena Partners, an enterprise involved in economic consultancy, specialising in international economic cooperation. He is also Research Associate of the Crawford School of

Economics and Government at the Australian National University and teaches at the University of Tasmania. From 1985 to 1987, Dr Elek served as Chief Economist in the Economic Planning Advisory Council of the Australian Government. From 1987 to 1990, he was Head of the Economic and Trade Development Division of the Department of Foreign Affairs and Trade. In 1989, he was the inaugural chairman of the APEC Senior Officials and had a central role in the establishment of the Asia-Pacific Economic Cooperation Process.

Peter Drysdale is Emeritus Professor of Economics and Visiting Fellow in Policy and Governance at the Crawford School of Economics and Government, the Australian National University. He is also regarded as the leading intellectual architect of APEC and won the Asia-Pacific Prize for his book, The Economics of International Economic Pluralism (1988). Until 2002, he was Executive Director of the Australia-Japan Research Centre. Professor Drysdale's main areas of expertise are international trade and economic policy; Australia's economic relations with East Asia and the Pacific; the East Asian and Japanese economy and economic policy and developments in Asia-Pacific economic integration. This work includes developments in Asia-Pacific economic cooperation; and relations between East Asia, Europe and APEC. His research work also extends to Chinese and Korean economies. Between 1984 and 1987, Professor Drysdale was Chairman of the Australian Pacific Economic Cooperation Committee (AUSPECC).

Charles E. Morrison has been President of the East-West Center, Honolulu, USA since 1 August 1998. He has had extensive involvement in the conceptualization, organization and funding of policy-oriented educational research and dialogue projects in both Japan and the United States, and has long been involved in promoting the concept of the Asia-Pacific community. In September 2005, Dr Morrison was elected international chair of the Pacific Economic Cooperation Council (PECC). He is a founding member of the U.S. Asia-Pacific Council, the U.S. National Committee for Pacific Economic Cooperation and is a member of the U.S. Committee for Security Cooperation in Asia Pacific. He is a past chair of the U.S. National Consortium of APEC Study Centers, a former director of the Center's Program on International Economics and Politics, and a former U.S. Senate aide and a research adviser to bi-national Japan-U.S. commissions.

Man-jung Mignonne Chan is Senior Advisor of the National Security Council in Chinese Taipei. Currently, she is on sabbatical leave from the Graduate School of American Studies at Tamkang University and also serves as APEC Expert on Individual Action Plans (IAPs). Dr Chan's career path traces a rare combination of academia, media, business, government and civil service of Asia-

Pacific regional organizations. Dr Chan has also served as Director-General of the PECC (Pacific Economic Cooperation Council) International Secretariat, Director (Research) at the APEC Secretariat, APEC IAP Expert and Chief of Staff for the Chinese Taipei ABAC (APEC Business Advisory Council).

Zhang Yunling is Professor, Academy Member, and Director of International Studies, Chinese Academy of Social Sciences (CASS) (2006- present), and President of the Chinese Association of Asia-Pacific Studies in the People's Republic of China. At CASS, he was also Director of the Institute of Asia-Pacific Studies (1993–2007). He is also a Member of the Chinese People's Political Consultative Conference (CPPCC, 2002–present), the East Asia Vision Group (EAVG, 2000–02), the Official Expert Group for China–ASEAN Cooperation (2001–02), and Chairman of the Joint Expert Group for Feasibility Studies on East Asia FTA (2004–06).

Shen Minghui is Assistant Research Fellow with the Institute of Asia-Pacific Studies at Chinese Academy of Social Sciences in the People's Republic of China. Dr Shen specializes in international economics.

Hadi Soesastro is senior fellow at the Centre for Strategic and International Studies (CSIS), Jakarta, Indonesia. Formerly he was Executive Director of CSIS as well as a member of the National Economic Council, an advisory council of former Indonesian President Abdurrahman Wahid. In July 2009, the Australian National University honoured Dr Hadi Soesastro for his achievements in promoting the idea of regionalism in East Asia and the Asia Pacific. He has also been instrumental in developing the Pacific Economic Cooperation Council (PECC). He is an Adjunct Professor at the Research School of Pacific & Asian Studies (RSPAS) of the Australian National University. In addition to lecturing at national universities, he has taught at Columbia University (New York). He is also on the editorial board of a number of international journals, including the *ASEAN Economic Bulletin* (Singapore) and the *Bulletin of Indonesian Economic Studies* (Canberra).

Ippei Yamazawa is Professor Emeritus, Hitotsubashi University, ex-President, International University of Japan (2003–06), and former President, Institute of Developing Economies /JETRO (1998–2003). He regularly participated in the Pacific Trade and Development Conference until 1999, and the Pacific Economic Cooperation Conference until 2003. Dr Yamazawa is Coordinator of APEC Study Center Japan Consortium (1995–present), a Member of the APEC Eminent Persons Group (1993–95), and Consultant on the APEC IAP peer review process (on Australia, 2002–03). He has published *Guidance to APEC* (in Japanese, co-authored with MOFA and MITI 1995), *APEC: Challenges and Tasks in the Twenty-First Century* (editor, 2000), and *Japan-ASEAN Comprehensive Economic Partnership: Vision and Agenda* 2003).

Tommy Koh is currently Ambassador-at-Large at the Ministry of Foreign Affairs, Singapore, Chairman of the National Heritage Board and of the Institute of Policy Studies (IPS). Together with Lee Tsao Yuan and Arun Mahizhnan, Professor Koh convened the first meeting of the Pacific Business Forum (PBF) in 1994, subsequently renamed as the APEC Business Council (ABAC). During 1994 and 1995, IPS served as the secretariat of PBF.

Lee Tsao Yuan is currently Coaching Practice Leader of SDC Consulting, a regional provider of Organizational Development and Human Resource training, consulting and coaching services. She sits on the board of the Singapore Land Authority. Previously, Dr Lee was on the board of the Overseas-Chinese Banking Corporation Ltd and Keppel Corporation Ltd (2001–09), NASDAQ-listed Pacific Internet Ltd (2000–05), Keppel Capital Holdings Ltd (2001) and Keppel FELS Energy and Infrastructure Ltd (1999–2001). She was Deputy Director of the Institute of Policy Studies in Singapore from 1990 to 1997, and Director from 1997–2000. She also participated as Singapore's only representative to the APEC Eminent Persons Group, and as Consultant to the Ministry of Foreign Affairs where she was directly involved in policy formulation associated with the hosting of the World Trade Organisation's Ministerial Meeting in Singapore 1996, as well as several APEC and ASEM meetings.

Arun Mahizhnan is Deputy Director at the Institute of Policy Studies (IPS), Singapore, in which he helped in setting the strategic direction of IPS, and overseeing its research output and the management of IPS. Mr Mahizhnan also leads the research work in the areas of Arts & Culture and Media at the Institute. His research interests also include business issues such as regionalization of the Singapore economy, the Pacific Business Forum, and development of entrepreneurship. He is concurrently an Adjunct Professor at the Wee Kim Wee School of Communication & Information at the Nanyang Technological University, Singapore. Before joining IPS in 1991, he worked in both the public and private sectors for 20 years, mostly in the filed of public communication.

Asia-Pacific Economic Cooperation (APEC)

2. The First APEC Ministerial Meeting, Canberra, Australia, 7–8 November 1989. APEC begins as an informal Ministerial-level dialogue with twelve members. *Photo courtesy of the APEC Secretariat.*

1

APEC: Genesis and Challenges

Andrew Elek

Introduction

Some of the foundations of APEC were laid more than 40 years ago. Careful consensus building, based on the achievements of ASEAN and PECC made it possible to launch APEC, based on agreed principles, in 1989. The process evolved quickly in its early years; by 1994 APEC leaders set themselves the remarkably ambitious objective of free and open trade.

Much has been achieved since then, but there have also been some disappointments. The first Bogor deadline of free and open trade and investment for developed APEC economies by 2010 will not be met.

Learning from experience, APEC now needs to act in line with the comparative advantage of a voluntary process of cooperation, rather than attempt to become a negotiating forum.

Some traditional border barriers remain. But the negotiations needed to reduce them can be left to the forums designed to conduct them. That would allow APEC to concentrate on issues which are of considerably greater concern to most of those involved in international commerce. These are practical matters like logistic constraints, inadequate communications, security concerns and the need to cope with different regulations in other economies.

APEC governments are already cooperating effectively in these areas. The constraints are lack of capacity, rather than political will. Voluntary cooperation has been proved to be feasible in these areas, but much more can be done.

APEC leaders could raise the profile of such important work by setting long-term targets in specific practical areas discussed in this paper. Achieving ambitious, but realistic, milestones on the way to such targets would allow APEC to transform itself to a process which records a sequence of realistic, ambitious and practical achievements, year after year.

Sadly, this is may not be possible. Instead of steady progress in line with the founding concepts of voluntary cooperation and open regionalism, many years may be wasted in an attempt to negotiate a lowest common denominator, APEC-wide trading bloc.

The Foundations of APEC

APEC builds on foundations which were laid more than 40 years ago. In the 1960s, the Pacific Trade and Development (PAFTAD) conferences started to assess the changing economic environment of the Asia Pacific. Its work was complemented by the Pacific Basin Economic Council (PBEC), a group of senior business people seeking to forge closer economic links in the region.

These groups analysed the growing, market-driven interdependence of Asia-Pacific economies with very different and often complementary resources. Some 57 per cent of exports and 55 per cent of imports of these economies were already traded within the region.

Some Asia-Pacific economies were already trading their way out of poverty and reducing obstacles to international trade and investment. Others, such as Indonesia, were engaging in the international economy, while China was beginning its "opening to the outside world". Each opening enhanced the competitiveness of the economy undertaking the reform and created new opportunities for other economies, encouraging further reform and promoting closer, mutually beneficial integration.

The work of PAFTAD highlighted the crucial role of the international trading system based on the General Agreement on Tariffs and Trade (GATT). The virtuous cycle which was leading to the relative increase in the Pacific region's share of global economic activity relied on confidence in such an open, rules-based and non-discriminatory trading system.

International consultations were seen to be needed in response to growing interdependence; to identify new opportunities for trade and investment and to anticipate potential tensions.

Since the 1960s, ASEAN had demonstrated that a voluntary association of diverse nations was possible. By 1980, its members had developed a strong sense of community and were able to project a powerful, collective influence in wider forums. ASEAN's success paved the way for policy-oriented discussions embracing the entire Asia-Pacific region.

Following careful consultations, the Pacific Economic Cooperation Council (PECC) was established in 1980. In addition to researchers and business people, it engaged government officials in discussions about international economic cooperation — at that stage in a personal capacity.

It was soon recognized that organizational models developed elsewhere could not be simply transplanted to the Asia Pacific, which would not accept a supra-national authority that could impose formal obligations on its governments. Therefore, cooperation would need to be voluntary, helping to identify and act on shared interests, rather than trying to create a negotiating forum.

PECC's analysis identified region-wide interests in investment policy, agriculture, minerals and energy, transport, telecommunications and tourism. Above all it underlined the benefits of sustained reform to reduce the costs and risks of international trade and investment.

Awareness of history and the importance of the region's global economic interests led to a firm rejection of a potential closed trading bloc modelled on the then European Community (Drysdale 2009). The consensus was to adopt open regionalism, seeking to reduce obstacles to closer economic integration in the Asia Pacific without seeking to divert economic activity away from the rest of the world.

The Hawke Initiative

Mutually beneficial interdependence proceeded apace in the 1980s, leading to progressively more serious proposals to involve Asia-Pacific governments.

By the late 1980s, the need for inter-governmental dialogues was becoming urgent.

The rapid relative rise of western Pacific economies placed great strains on the GATT system as competition from these newly successful economies forced structural adjustment on others. Throughout the 1980s, they were taking market shares from labour-intensive industries across the Pacific, triggering protectionist responses such as the United States' Super 301 legislation (Drysdale 1990).

The current drift away from a multilateral non-discriminatory approach to trade had already begun. The United States had just concluded a bilateral trading arrangement with Canada; a significant departure from its role as the champion of non-discriminatory trade. In 1989, there was fear of a "Fortress Europe", reinforced by the willingness of Europe to allow the Montreal mid-term review of the Uruguay Round to fail.

In the late 1980s, Pacific leaders were still prepared to defend the post-war, non-discriminatory trading system. Their search for a way to protect the region's overriding interest in a rules-based multilateral trading system prompted several initiatives.

Tentative options were floated by former Japanese Prime Minister Yasuhiro Nakasone, then by the US Secretary of State, George Shultz. US Senator Bill Bradley called for a trans-Pacific alliance to defend the multilateral trading system. In late 1988, PECC recommended that regional consultations be elevated to inter-governmental level.

PECC's experience had encouraged Australian Prime Minister Bob Hawke to initiate a series of meetings of Western Pacific trade ministers to define their shared interest in launching the Uruguay Round of GATT negotiations. Later in the 1980s, PECC had also pioneered the way for policy-oriented economic consultations to include both the People's Republic of China and Chinese Taipei.[1]

By early 1988, Australia's Department of Foreign Affairs and Trade (DFAT) and Japan's Ministry of International Trade and Industry (MITI) were exploring options for a ministerial level Meeting. MITI's report on potential Asia-Pacific economic cooperation warned against a world economy divided into trading blocs. It called for a new form of regionalism in the region, which should not be inward-looking and discriminatory, but based on the concept of open regionalism (MITI, 1998).

DFAT also submitted a report to the government on options for regional economic cooperation, recommending an early initiative to capitalize on a self-confident mood in East Asia and the need to re-engage the United States in collective leadership of the multilateral trading system. The report also stressed the need to learn from the experience and knowledge accumulated by ASEAN, PAFTAD and PECC.

The history of these institutions suggested that all successful cooperation in the Asia-Pacific region needed to be based on principles of:

- Openness to wider participation, together with non-discrimination and transparency in trade and economic policy.
- Equal respect for all participants, leading to activities of mutual benefit, while anticipating rapid transformation in the structure of economic and political power in the region.
- An evolutionary, pragmatic approach towards closer regional cooperation based on consensus-building and voluntary participation.[2]

Hawke was able to build on these foundations. Following consultation with Korean President Roh Tae Woo, he launched what became APEC in Seoul, on 31 January 1989. Hawke sought support for a process of analysis and consultation among governments help strengthen the multilateral trading system, to assess prospects for increased trade and investment flows and to identify common economic interests in the Asia-Pacific region. He suggested that regional cooperation could draw on the experience of the OECD, while ruling out the prospect of an Asia-Pacific trading bloc.

The Road to Canberra

The initial reaction from the region was positive, but cautious. An intense process of consultations by Australian officials around the region, led by Secretary of DFAT, Richard Woolcott, served to define the objectives and the nature of a process of cooperation which would suit the needs of the extremely diverse Asia Pacific.[3]

The ASEAN economies were the first to be consulted in detail, starting in Indonesia. Discussions with President Soeharto, several ministers and senior officials proved invaluable while warning of strict speed limits on the evolution of inter-governmental cooperation. Singapore's Prime Minister Lee Kuan Yew was keen to proceed.

By the end of Woolcott's consultations with ASEAN, there was firm consensus that any economic cooperation in the region should be outward-looking, not defensive. The region's prosperity depended on worldwide, not just Pacific, trading links. Therefore any new initiative should not become a trading bloc.

It was also agreed that the shape of the process should not be dictated by the currently most powerful. Giving due weight to the views of all participants made it essential that cooperation be voluntary, building consensus on a gradually wider range of economic issues, rather than a negotiating forum.

It was accepted that a sequence of productive ministerial-level meetings would need to be backed up by professional analytical work. Instead of setting up a new bureaucracy, existing organizations like PECC should provide the necessary support.

The discussions in Japan were challenging. MITI was extremely eager to launch a new initiative, but the Ministry of Foreign Affairs was very reluctant. This problem was resolved, fortuitously, when the Minister for Foreign Affairs became Prime Minister, and the MITI Minister became the new Minister for Foreign Affairs in mid-1989.

China's strong preference was to include only sovereign states. However, the door was left open to the potential participation of Hong Kong and Taiwan, provided the process was defined to be a high-level forum for consultations among economies. The tragic events of 4 June 1989 made it impossible to resolve the participation of the three Chinese economies in 1989. Following delicate negotiations, they joined APEC in November 1991.[4]

Across the Pacific, Canada was anxious to join and the United States confirmed its support during Hawke's June visit. At the ASEAN post-ministerial consultation in early July 1989, ASEAN agreed to participate in an exploratory ministerial-level meeting in Canberra in November.

The consensus which had been achieved on the nature of potential cooperation, was summed up, as follows, in a note sent to potential participants by Woolcott on completion of his consultations:

- Any new initiative should build on existing foundations: in particular, ASEAN's identity and cohesion should be preserved.
- Cooperation should be based on the principles of equality, equity and mutual benefit, taking account of the differences in stages of economic development and socio-political systems.

- Cooperation should not be directed towards the formation of an inward-looking economic or trading bloc. On the contrary, any cooperation should strengthen the open multilateral economic and trading system.
- Any new forum should be consultative, rather than seek to impose mandatory directives.
- Cooperation should enhance the capacity of participants for economic analysis to enable participants to identify and pursue common interests, including in larger multilateral forums.
- The process should proceed gradually and pragmatically, especially in its institutionalisation, without inhibiting further elaboration and future expansion.
- Participation would be open to others who accepted the above principles, to be decided by consensus of existing participants.

In an August 1989 article in the *Far Eastern Economic Review*, Jusuf Wanandi listed conditions under which ASEAN might be prepared to engage in ongoing cooperation.[5] These were essentially consistent with the above and were endorsed at the first-ever APEC senior officials meeting held in Sydney in mid-September 1989.[6] Officials agreed on an agenda for the proposed meeting which struck a balance between prejudgment of outcomes and the wish to see the Canberra meeting as the beginning of a substantive, ongoing process.

From Canberra to Bogor

The first ministerial-level meeting confirmed the will to initiate an ongoing process of cooperation. A cordial and collegial atmosphere allowed a very brief Joint Statement of Ministers to be drafted during the meeting, rather than negotiated beforehand. In that statement, ministers acknowledged:

> … the important contribution ASEAN and its dialogue relationships have played in the development to date of APEC.

The statement noted that none of the ministers believed:

> that Asia-Pacific Economic Cooperation should be directed to the formation of a trading bloc.

They agreed that:

> … it was premature at this stage to decide on any particular structure either for a Ministerial-level forum or its necessary support mechanism, but that — while ideas were evolving — it was appropriate for further consultative meetings to take place and work to be undertaken on matters of common interest and concern.

Following discussion of opportunities to cooperate on specific issues, consensus was reached on nine basic principles of the APEC process, based on the ideas which had been put forward by Wanandi and Woolcott.

Ministers agreed to meet again in Singapore in 1990, then in Seoul in 1991. The APEC process was under way, expanding its membership to 21 economies by 1997.

The first important step after the Canberra meeting was taken in Kuching in early 1990, where ASEAN economic ministers defined the conditions for ASEAN's continued partnership in the APEC process. This Kuching Consensus, which remains valid today, is once again based very closely on Wanandi's proposals, hence consistent with those affirmed at the initial meeting of APEC Ministers. They were subsequently reaffirmed and elaborated in the 1991 Seoul APEC Declaration which set out the objectives, scope of activity, mode of operation, participation and organization of the new process.

An initial work programme was agreed in Singapore, in 1990. By 1993, there was sufficient confidence in the process to begin annual summit meetings of APEC economic leaders. The 1994 meeting of APEC leaders, in Bogor adopted the goal of free and open trade and investment. This was to be achieved by developed and developing APEC economies eliminating obstacles to trade and investment by 2010 and 2020, respectively.

The 2005 Osaka Action Agenda set out a blueprint for liberalizing border barriers, combined with efforts to facilitate trade and investment by reducing many other costs and risks of international commerce. Liberalization and facilitation were to be backed by economic and technical co-operation to enhance the capacity to design and implement the necessary reforms.

Some Achievements

Concerted decisions of APEC governments to reduce obstacles to trade and investment have sustained the "opening to the outside world" which was underway by 1989. The Asia Pacific continues to be the most open and dynamic region in the world.

By the time of the 2005 mid-term stocktake of progress:

- average tariffs were considerably lower than in 1989 and there were few quantitative restrictions on trade. Border barriers to trade in many goods were already set at zero or negligible levels.
- people and capital were moving more freely around the region.
- more efficient customs procedures, progress towards paperless trading, mutual recognition of standards and other practical arrangements to facilitate trade and investment were already saving billions of dollars per year.
- an APEC initiative in the WTO ensured that information technology (IT) products have remained freely traded.

It is very hard to isolate the contribution of APEC to the reforms by individual governments which led to these achievements. The difficulty of allocating credit is compounded by the voluntary nature of APEC, which means that decisions of governments are not mandated by, or directly attributable to the APEC process. But there is no doubt that APEC has made a useful contribution to the success of the region.

The willingness to share information, experience, expertise and technology, accompanied by a willingness to accept peer pressure to act in line with agreed commitments, has proved valuable. Such cooperation is particularly effective in dealing with non-border impediments to trade, such as customs procedures, where collective action is essentially a matter of capacity-building to implement shared objectives. APEC's work in these areas, which is its comparative advantage, has made it a world leader in terms of facilitating trade and investment.

The APEC process has also generated a habit of mutual respect and consultation by officials and political leaders of the region. This helped to entrench a shared commitment to openness that was sustained through the financial crisis of the late 1990s. Sharing experience and expertise has helped Asia Pacific governments to respond to threats like international terrorism and the SARS epidemic, with minimal damage to trade and investment flows.

The APEC process has helped to integrate China into the WTO and the international economy and the annual summits of economic leaders provide many opportunities to think about, anticipate, or defuse potential problems.

Some Disappointments

There have also been some disappointments, partly due to discord about the nature of the process and unrealistic expectations.

An Eminent Persons Group (EPG), appointed to recommend strategic options, was influential in setting the 1994 Bogor Goals. The Bogor Declaration has provided APEC with a general sense of direction, but the EPG was not able to define the meaning of free and open trade and investment, or to agree on the means for achieving it.

The overwhelming majority of the EPG favoured voluntary cooperation to make progress towards the Bogor Goals, with both liberalization and facilitation to be backed by technical cooperation and capacity-building. By contrast, the Chairman (Fred Bergsten) perceived APEC to be a trade organisation, whose central objective was to become a trading bloc. Voluntary cooperation was eventually adopted as the means to implement the Osaka Action Agenda, but it was not possible to resolve the debate about whether trade liberalisation was to be preferential or non-discriminatory. And, until quite recently, far too little attention has been given to capacity-building.

Although the Osaka Action Agenda is quite broad, there has been undue emphasis on traditional border barriers to trade in goods, which are relatively easy to measure and understand. Inevitably, the declaration that free and open trade and investment was to be achieved by

2010/2020 raised the expectation that APEC could bring about substantial reductions of protection of sensitive products. This was an extraordinarily ambitious goal for liberalization (Patrick 2005). Not even the European Union has achieved anything like free trade in services among its members. Nor has the WTO ever set itself the objective of eliminating all obstacles to trade and investment.

Creating an unrealistic expectation for trade liberalization has haunted the process since 1994. By the late 1990s, concerted unilateral liberalization had led to very significant reductions on border barriers. However, it could also be seen that voluntary cooperation was not going to be adequate to deal with some sensitive products, like agriculture, textiles and clothing. These are the same products which are proving impossible to eliminate in the near future, either in the WTO, or in preferential trading arrangements.

Looking Ahead

It is now evident that the 2010 deadline for trade liberalization is not going to be reached by concerted unilateral liberalization. There is ongoing pressure to convert APEC to a process which could impose binding decisions on participants, which would require a revision of APEC's agreed guiding principles. This pressure is accompanied by the ongoing debate about turning APEC into yet another trading bloc, which would also require revisiting the agreed principles.

An Asia-Pacific Trading Bloc?

The so-called early voluntary sectoral liberalization (EVSL) experiment in conducting trade negotiations among APEC governments failed dismally in 1998. Nevertheless, APEC governments may yet be persuaded to do something far more difficult and try to negotiate an APEC-wide trading bloc.

Any such negotiations would be a drawn-out process, which would need to overcome huge political obstacles. For example, a meaningful agreement involving the United States and major East Asian economies would require a significant renegotiation of the rules of origin of NAFTA, which are designed to avoid new competition from East Asian imports of sensitive products. The political difficulty of such reforms is quite likely to lead to an obvious failure like the attempted Free Trade Area of the Americas (FTAA).

One way to dodge around the difficult decisions needed for a comprehensive agreement would be settle for a lowest common denominator FTAAP, with many sensitive products exempted from the deal. Such an agreement would certainly not bring about free trade and investment.

Even in the narrow terms of liberalizing border barriers, the Asia Pacific would still be well short of where the EU was by 1970. During the many years of negotiations, progress on behind-the-border obstacles to trade would grind to a halt while APEC governments negotiated a single undertaking leading to a possible FTAAP. Progress on important new issues would, as in the WTO, be held hostage to the lobbying power of the producers of a few sensitive products accounting for a rapidly shrinking share of international trade.

Any potential FTAAP would not, in itself, achieve substantive progress on non-border issues. As the experience of recent preferential trade agreements shows, it is possible to negotiate statements of good intentions and committees to study them. However, tangible progress is a matter of patient design of institutions and policies, backed by capacity building, which cannot be created by negotiations.

Despite these problems, or perhaps due to a refusal to acknowledge them, some members of ABAC and, in 2006, a remarkably inept United States administration have supported the idea of an APEC trading bloc. The idea has come to be described as no more than a long-term prospect, but continues to divert attention from pursuing a more realistic strategy in line with the comparative advantage of a voluntary process of cooperation.

As set out in the 2005 stocktake of progress (APEC, 2005), voluntary cooperation has promoted very significant trade and investment facilitation. But much more could be done. Due to inadequate high-level attention, the APEC process has yet to catalyse the resources needed to create the capacity for efficient logistics and communications and the many other investments needed to reduce the costs and risks of international commerce in the Asia Pacific.

Accepting Reality

The challenge of reducing obstacles to trade and investment is open-ended: for example, there will always be scope for improving the efficiency of ports and airports. In other words, the full elimination of border barriers by a given date is theoretically possible, but politically too hard; while the challenge of facilitation to eliminate other costs and risks in trade and investment is never-ending. Fully free and open trade and investment is a useful ideal, but it will never be reached.

Without some imaginative reorientation, APEC risks a perception of always falling short of self-imposed deadlines which cannot be met.

Despite all its achievements, the majority of those who assess APEC are frustrated with its performance, relative to the Bogor goal of free and open trade and investment. This frustration is also diverting attention from APEC towards preferential trading arrangements and East Asian initiatives for cooperation. APEC's survival and potential impact in the coming years will depend on whether it proves possible to create synergy among trans-Pacific and East Asian forums.

APEC's relevance will also depend on its prospects to facilitate ongoing rapid structural adjustment. In recent years, the Economic Committee of APEC has developed an agenda to enhance the efficiency of domestic markets and other institutional dimensions of structural adjustment. This promises to be a useful complement to APEC's ongoing work on trade and investment facilitation.

The economic integration agenda will also need to avoid further preoccupation with border barriers and to focus the nature of economic integration in 2009.

The Changing Nature of International Commerce

Economic integration in the 21st century is driven largely by market signals, rather than by inter-governmental trading arrangements. At a time when most goods and services face no, or very low, formal trade barriers, those traditional barriers are no longer the strategic impediments to economic integration. These days, the problems of most concern of those engaged in international commerce are:

- weak logistics,
- inadequate communications, especially the electronic exchange of data,
- coping with security concerns; and
- different, not always transparent, regulations in other economies.

In the light of these new realities, the current challenge is to complement a world of already low border barriers to trade in most products with an environment of:

- *national treatment of investment;*
- *well-managed financial systems;*
- *transparency, best practice, and consistency of regulations, including:*
    - *competition policy,*
    - *regulations on government procurement.*
- *mutual recognition of standards and qualifications;*
- *efficient communications, including paperless e-commerce;*
- *best practice logistics.*[7]

Due to the current lack of human, physical and institutional capacity in many Asia-Pacific economies, the region as a whole is a long way from these essential characteristics of genuine free and open trade and investment. On the other hand, some APEC economies, for example Singapore, have already created several dimensions of such an environment. These front-runners can help others to catch up to what they have already done.

To a large extent, creating the environment described above among diverse economies involves helping those that want to adapt current best practice by sharing information, experience, expertise and technology. For example, APEC economies with the most efficient ports and airports could share their experience to improve those of others.

The gains from such initiatives would be enormous. For example:

- the Asian Development Bank has noted the potential to save up to 1 per cent of the value of traded products by reducing port clearance times by just one day.
- research by the World Bank (2007)

has estimated that bringing below average APEC members half way to the APEC average in terms of the efficiency of their trade logistics would result in a 10 per cent increase in intra-APEC trade, worth about US$280 billion.

The constraint on effective collective action to realize these potential gains is not political will, but the capacity to design and implement compatible institutions and procedures. Progress does not depend on negotiations, but on the willingness to share information, experience, expertise and technology. Therefore collective action on matters such enhancing the efficiency and security of supply chains is in line with the comparative advantage APEC.

Once adequate attention is paid to the current nature of economic integration, the 20th birthday of APEC can be an opportunity to recover credibility and become a process which can record the achievement of realistic targets with practical benefits to the private sector directly involved in international trade and investment.

This is also a time to reaffirm the concept of open regionalism: to deal with the remaining challenges of genuine economic integration, without seeking to discriminate against the Asia Pacific's important trading partners in the rest of the world. There is no need to pursue the faint hope of a lowest common denominator FTAAP. APEC can concentrate on implementing the strategy adopted in 2005.

Reviving the Busan Roadmap

Following an assessment of progress in 2005, APEC leaders endorsed a Busan Roadmap designed to sustain momentum towards free and open trade and investment.

The Busan Roadmap accepted that APEC is not a negotiating forum and offered the hope of a sound division of effort between APEC and the WTO, consistent with their comparative advantage. Issues which needed negotiations, particularly the remaining border barriers to sensitive products, could be left to the WTO, which is designed as a negotiating forum. APEC could then concentrate on the issues of immediate concern to business. Accordingly, the heart of the new roadmap for APEC was the Busan Business Agenda.

This agenda reflected the changing environment for international commerce and responded to repeated calls by ABAC (2004, 2005) for APEC governments to take concerted action to deal with issues such as customs procedures, standards and conformance, business mobility, e-commerce, secure trade logistics, transparency and anti-corruption, intellectual property rights, sound financial systems and competition policy.

Without need for negotiations, APEC has already helped member economies to make worthwhile progress in all these fields. Sustaining this momentum, a second phase of the Trade Facilitation Action Plan is now being implemented to reduce transactions costs by a further 5 per cent. Under Singapore leadership, close attention is being given to practical ways of reducing transport and communications costs.

At the same time, much more could be done with commitment to specific targets, which are realistic as well as ambitious, combined with a commitment to help mobilize the resources needed to invest in the necessary capacity-building. Such targets could include:

- mutual recognition and testing of standards and qualifications, comparable in scope to that achieved by the EU;
- full compatibility of customs and security clearance procedures, and electronic interchange of relevant data;
- transparency and harmonization of a wide range of other administrative procedures;
- region-wide minimum standards for competition policy, to reduce the need for anti-dumping actions among APEC economies.
- bringing the efficiency of all Asia Pacific ports and airports much closer to best practice.

It will take many years to approach such ambitious objectives. But APEC leaders can adopt realistic medium-term milestones to be achieved along the way. Attaining such milestones for progress could allow APEC to record a sequence of tangible achievements, year after year.

Notes

1. Details of PECC's contribution can be found in Woods (1993), Terada (1999) and Elek (2005*a*).
2. These principles of openness, equality and evolution were first expressed in Drysdale (1988).
3. Woolcott (2003) and Elek (2005*b*) provide a more detailed account of the process of consultations leading to the first meeting of APEC Ministers.
4. Based on the formula agreed in PECC, the three are designated as China, Chinese Taipei and Hong Kong, China.
5. See also Wanandi (1989).
6. The name "Asia Pacific Economic Cooperation" was used for the first time at this meeting, chaired by the author.
7. This list of desirable characteristics for the Asia-Pacific region draws on the list presented by Robert R. Romulo, a member of ABAC, in July 2005.

References

ABAC (APEC Business Advisory Council). "A single market agenda for the Asia Pacific". ABAC, Australia, *Contribution to Discussion on the FTAAP Proposal*, August 2004.

ABAC. *Networking the Asia Pacific: A Pathway to Common Prosperity*. Report to APEC economic leaders, October 2005.

APEC. "A mid-term stocktake of progress towards the Bogor Goals: Busan Roadmap to Bogor Goals". Report by APEC senior officials, 2005.

Drysdale, Peter. "Australia's Asia-Pacific economic diplomacy". *Current Affairs Bulletin* 66, no. 10 (1990).

———. *International Economic Pluralism*. Sydney: Allen & Unwin, 1988.

Drysdale, Peter. Chapter 2 in this volume.

Elek, Andrew. "The Birth of PECC: the Canberra Seminar". In *The Evolution of PECC: The First 25 Years*. Singapore:

Pacific Economic Cooperation Council (PECC) International Secretariat, 2005*a*.

Elek, Andrew. "Back to Canberra: Founding APEC". In *The Evolution of PECC: The First 25 Years*. Singapore: Pacific Economic Cooperation Council (PECC) International Secretariat, 2005*b*.

MITI (Ministry of International Trade and Industry). "Aratanaru Ajia Taiheiyou Kyoryoku-wo Motomete" [Towards A New Asia Pacific Cooperation]. Tokyo: MITI, 1988.

Patrick, Hugh. "PECC, APEC and East Asian Economic Cooperation: Prime Minister Ohira's Legacy and Issues of the 21st Century". *The Evolution of PECC: The First 25 Years*. PECC, Singapore, 2005.

Romulo, R. "ABAC inputs to the 2006 APEC agenda". Presentation on behalf of ABAC to the International Symposium on the Preparation for APEC Viet Nam 2006. Ha Noi, July 2005.

Terada, Takashi. "Creating an Asia Pacific Economic Community: The Roles of Australia and Japan in regional institution-building". Ph D dissertation, Australian National University, submitted February 1999.

Woolcott, Richard. *The Hot Seat: Reflections on Diplomacy from Stalin's Death to the Bali Bombings*. Sydney: Harper and Collins, 2003.

Woods, Lawrence. *Asia-Pacific Diplomacy: Nongovernmental Organizations and International Relations*. Vancouver: UBC Press, 1993.

Wanandi, Jusuf. "The role of PECC in the 1990s and Pacific institutions". Occasional Papers, M6/89. Jakarta: Center for Strategic and International Studies, 1989.

World Bank. *Connecting to Compete — Trade Logistics in the Global Economy: The Logistics Performance Index and its Indicators*. Washington, DC, 2007.

3. This was the First Senior Officials meeting held in Jakarta in 1994. Working under direction from APEC Ministers, Senior Officials guide the activities of the Committees, Working Groups and Task Forces. Senior Officials develop recommendations for APEC Ministers and APEC Economic Leaders. The year 1994 was also significant when in November the APEC leaders set the Bogor Goals. *Photo courtesy of the APEC Secretariat.*

4. The APEC Leaders' Summits were the highlights in each APEC year. Here Prime Minister Goh is seen arriving at the Ninoy Aquino International Airport for the fourth APEC Summit in November 1996. *Photo courtesy of the APEC Secretariat.*

5. *Left*: The late President Soeharto of Indonesia being greeted by Japanese Prime Minister Tomiichi Murayama during the APEC Economic Leaders' Meeting in Osaka, Japan, in November 1995. *Photo courtesy of the APEC Secretariat*.

6. *Below*: President Jiang Zemin of the People's Republic of China and Vice-President Al Gore of the United States of America at the APEC Economic Leaders' Meeting in Osaka, Japan, in November 1995. *Photo courtesy of the APEC Secretariat*.

7. APEC Economic Leaders' Meeting, Blake Island, 20 November 1993. At this meeting, leaders seized the opportunity to share their vision which led to the Bogor Declaration in 1994. *Photo courtesy of the APEC Secretariat.*

2

APEC's Origins and its Future*

Peter Drysdale

The idea of Asia-Pacific Economic Cooperation (APEC) has evolved over the years, but it continues to be rooted in the reality of the complex political and economic circumstance of the Asia-Pacific economy and polity. Since 1989, when APEC was founded, the institution has changed profoundly. Since 1993, the leaders have met annually and these meetings bring weight to APEC's trans-Pacific political and economic dialogues. The East Asian financial crisis re-focused APEC's economic agenda, albeit more slowly than some might have wished, away from trade liberalization towards financial and other behind-the-border reform. Now the global financial crisis and the longer-term change in the structure of regional and global economic power call for a new look at how APEC might serve its members down the track. Recalling its origins and the processes on which it is built are the first step in considering how APEC might move forward in the years ahead.

Genesis

Although the theoretical underpinnings for an Asia-Pacific community were documented with remarkable prescience by Sir John Crawford as early as 1938, the road towards the establishment of Asia-Pacific Economic Cooperation (APEC) was long and there were many vicissitudes on the way. The idea of APEC was wrought from East Asia's rapid industrialization after the conclusion of the Pacific War. Industrialization created new, and powerful, interactions between East Asia and North America which, in turn, demanded the creation of a new framework for the relationship, first between the United States and Japan, and gradually between America and the whole region, prominently now, China. The debate about what form and function these new relationships should assume was painstaking because the effect that growing regional economic interdependence might have on the East Asian political economy was still uncertain (Woolcott 2003).

The objective was to secure and promote economic cooperation among the wider and wider group of economies in Asia and the Pacific that were becoming more deeply involved in the regional and international economy. Three factors conspired to set the context that shaped the formation of APEC. The first was the Asia Pacific's political, cultural and institutional diversity. This led, in conjunction with the burden of imperial history (including Japan's occupation of a large part of East Asia and its wartime aggression), to a certain agoraphobia in developing nations who would jealously guard their economic sovereignty, which initially limited broad and deep interaction among governments and community leaders in the region. Second, the Asia Pacific was a region that included economies at many stages of economic development, many of them newly committed to the process of reform and integration into the international economy. Third, and perhaps most saliently, America, a global power with global engagements, was initially not interested in the idea. In the final analysis, regional goals and policy priorities had to be patiently synergized (Funabashi 1995; Drysdale 1988), and a great deal of innovative thinking was invested in the engineering of a new form of regionalism which would fit the circumstances of the Asia Pacific.

The promoters of an Asia-Pacific inter-governmental organization were policy-oriented economists, business leaders, officials and politicians, and its design took over two decades to materialize. Momentum for APEC built throughout the 1970s and 80s. What had begun, in the late 1960s, as an academic and business network for the promotion of Asia-Pacific economic cooperation through the Pacific Trade Development (PAFTAD) conferences and the Pacific Basin Economic Council (PBEC) slowly evolved, by the late 1970s, into a larger community, including government officials, with greater influence over policy thinking (Donowaki 1982). This saw, by September 1980, the inauguration of the quasi-governmental Pacific Economic Cooperation Council (PECC). PECC, in turn, played a pivotal role in laying the foundations for the establishment of APEC (Soesastro 1994). Japan, having emerged as a major industrial power over the course of its recovery from the Pacific War, was at the forefront of this process. So was Australia because of its importance as a resource supplier to the region, and, together with America and Japan, formed another hub from which sprang APEC's various new, triangulated economic relationships.

Form and Function

The nature of economic cooperation arrangements in East Asia and the Pacific was shaped by the reality that, in this region, the power of market forces had to triumph over diversity; importantly, political diversity. These circumstances demanded a way of thinking which stressed the desire for both economic and political inclusiveness, and which resulted in the idea of "open regionalism" as the central theme on which APEC was based (Garnaut 1996). Open regionalism featured prominently in the conclusions of the ANU seminar which led to the establishment of PECC. There were (and still are), however, competing conceptions of regional cooperation earlier inspired, predominantly, by the example of Europe but, later, also by NAFTA. Although the emergence of the European community was a catalyst for the first serious regional discussion of options for Asia-Pacific economic cooperation at the PAFTAD conference in Tokyo in January 1968, the original proposal of a discriminatory Pacific Free Trade Area met with universal criticism (Arndt 1967). It was the European model which inspired discussion of an economic cooperation tailored to fit the Asia-Pacific circumstance but it was accepted that the European experience of increasing economic interdependence took place under quite different conditions.

Open regionalism involved commitment by a regional coalition to multilateral trade liberalization and to strengthening the policy and other infrastructure necessary to support trade-oriented economic development. At the outset APEC eschewed a discriminatory approach to comprehensive regional trade liberalization because that was thought to be both unfeasible and contrary to the global market interests of East Asian and Pacific countries. None of the major players, at that stage, were prepared to enter into a fully-fledged free trade area or common market since these strategies were inconsistent with regional circumstances and interests. Article 1 of the GATT/WTO, which establishes most favoured nation (MFN) as an overarching principle in the conduct of international trade, was at the heart of APEC's founding ideals. It, firstly, provided the newly industrializing economies of East Asia with an important measure of protection against the kind of discrimination that had previously haunted the international trade system, and secondly, ensured equality amongst the nations of East Asia and the Pacific, thereby acting to guarantee the political element in the paradigm of open regionalism.

Unilateral trade liberalization and economic reform became a major commitment of the economies in East Asia and Australasia from the late 1980s until the mid-1990s. These reforms provided the impetus for strong regional trade and economic growth, and ushered the East Asian hemisphere into its role as a new pole of growth and influence in the world economy (Drysdale and Garnaut 1993). These developments complemented the interests of, and approaches in, Southeast Asia (Ariff 1994;

Yamazawa 1992), and, when considered in conjunction with those interests, were influential in encouraging APEC leaders to commit to the Bogor Goals in Indonesia in 1994.

The Bogor Goals provided a target for trade and investment liberalization in the region by 2010 for developed countries, and by 2020 for developing countries. This provided regional players with the destination, but still left the path undefined. Thus, in the years following the 1994 Bogor conference competing conceptions of the way forward with regional cooperation began to emerge.

One main characteristic of APEC is its laissez-faire enforcement mechanism. There is no over-arching supra-national authority that governs APEC or any aspect of its member's economic policies. The APEC process deliberately avoids impinging on its members' sovereignty. Its importance and influence, and where it lies, derives entirely from consultation and persuasion in order to encourage commitment to regional goals and policy cooperation. Given the differences in values, rules, economic and political systems, social understandings and national aspirations in the Asia-Pacific region, consultative processes and institutions play an enormously valuable role in the gradual development of consistent and productive regional agendas (Harris 1994).

By some standards, which prioritize policies around binding rules and legal institutions, the structure and the mode of APEC appear weak (Kahler 1988; Aggarwal 1993; Higgott 1994). One criticism of the Bogor Declaration, for example, is that it is neither legally binding nor precisely defined. Yet, from another perspective, this characteristic of APEC can be considered its greatest strength. It has helped encourage widespread and representative participation in APEC from countries in the Asia-Pacific region. Considerable progress that otherwise would have been unlikely (Terada 2001), has been possible by at once both ensuring the economic sovereignty of member states, and promoting the convergence of policy on issues of importance to the regional economy.

East Asia's trade diplomacy was closely aligned to the multilateral system and the policy priority of non-discrimination in international trade. Notwithstanding increasingly interdependent economic and political interests within the Asia-Pacific region, the diversity of economies, societies and polities in the region meant that the theories and methods of economic integration which had served Europe and America so well did not correlate with the East Asian experience. Imitating European or North American foreign economic diplomacy in the Asia Pacific seemed to make no sense (Garnaut 1996; Bonnor 1996; Petri 1994). This is because the Asia Pacific's economic and political ambitions are ordered around the goal of modernization, and, furthermore, that members of APEC are located at both ends of the continuum along which politico-economic development is measured. Developing economies have a profound stake in a trade regime which prioritizes trade-equality because their trade and economic growth depends upon taking over market share from established suppliers to international markets. If the principle of non-discrimination in international trade continues to abrogated, developing East Asian economies will face obstacles to market access and their modernization through deeper integration into the international community would be markedly inhibited.

East Asian intraregional trade has been growing steadily, and it will continue to grow, but the geographical compass of East Asia's trading interests remains global. The East Asian market is, itself, getting bigger, but it cannot supply all of East Asia's materials, provide an outlet for all of East Asia's exports, or serve East Asia's international commercial or financial needs independently of the global economy, certainly not in light of China's persistently phenomenal annual increase in both imports from and exports to the rest of the world. Until recently around 30 per cent or more of East Asia's trade had been with the United States. Thus, East Asia's interests in the international system derive from the global spread of East Asia's economic interests. This reality has been underlined, not qualified by the current global financial and economic crisis.

This explains why APEC endeavoured to promote trade liberalization on a non-discriminatory basis, eschewing preferential trading arrangements in favour of promoting open regionalism (Elek 1992). These policies allowed the APEC community to accommodate East Asia's burgeoning economic power without disturbing the role played by North America in regional economic and political affairs. There was thus a convenient coincidence of multilateral economic and regional political interests which encouraged open regionalism based on a truly global agenda. East Asia gained a platform for representing and projecting its global economic interests and the United States was able to safeguard its security framework in the region.

Thus, although debate persisted regarding whether APEC needed to emulate European or North American regionalism, or whether it needed a new form of distinctly East Asian cooperation, there was early and significant progress with unilateral trade liberalisation in the region. China, on its route towards accession to the WTO, affirmed its historic commitment to trade reform at the APEC leaders meeting at Osaka in 1995.

The doubts about whether volunteerism could be sustained grew, however, when the attempt to pursue early voluntary sectoral liberalization at the Kuala Lumpur meetings in 1998 failed (Wesley 2001). The ensuing collapse of confidence in multilateral strategies through the East Asian financial crisis reinforced these doubts (Aggarwal and Morrison 2000; Ravenhill 2000). It was against this backdrop that the East Asian regional arrangements came to find new favour. The global financial crisis again has raised these doubts although, interestingly, through the G-20 process has at last propelled Asian leaders to a more global stance and role.

Evolution of the Idea

There were always several different and competing conceptions of East Asian and Pacific regionalism which had existed since the outset. One related to what constituted the appropriate membership of an Asia-Pacific regional organization, and the other related to the mode of regional cooperation that the regional organization should adopt. For example, when Australian Prime Minister Bob Hawke proposed what became the APEC initiative in 1989, the concept did not include North America. Rather, the conceptualization of APEC lent the idea momentum which catalysed American interest and participation in the initiative.

Later, although the idea of an emerging East Asian economic bloc did not originally sit well with the nature of economic relations among the East Asian economies and their relationship with the rest of the world, the argument for institutionalizing APEC in the form of a Free Trade Area of the Asia Pacific (FTAAP) was always stirring just below the surface. How to resolve or relate these competing conceptualizations is now a major issue for APEC.

The last decade of the twentieth century saw a marked shift in thinking about regional cooperation in East Asia and the Pacific driven by both economic and political forces (Bergsten 2000). The shift in the status quo which triggered the emergence of the new regionalism in East Asia arose at the time of the 1997 East Asian financial crisis. Whereas earlier former Prime Minister Mahathir of Malaysia proposed the formation of an East Asian Economic Caucus to no avail, the circumstances in the late 1990s were quite different. Partly driven by the complex political response to Washington's role in dealing with the 1997 financial crisis, and partly because of a loss of faith in APEC's capacity to deal with contemporary financial problems, a more exclusively East Asian regionalism and preferential trading initiatives gained sway. Coupled with the failure to launch a new WTO round of trade negotiations in Seattle, which had been so central to APEC's trade liberalization agenda (Aggarwal 2001), these developments came to justify heading in a new direction through the enterprise of ASEAN+3, and the negotiation of bilateral preferential trade arrangements in East Asia (Soesastro 2001; Tay 2001). Thus, the APEC region, in the late twentieth century, was characterized by burgeoning preferentialism and bilateralism in trade and economic policy.

The East Asian financial crisis provided an imperative for deeper financial and trade cooperation within East Asia. However, Japan's own domestic financial market was hit hard by the crisis, and its call for an Asian Monetary Fund then met with little support, even within the East Asian region. Japan had no capacity to avert the US retreat from a new WTO round in Seattle, and impetus on the issue of trade liberalization within the framework of APEC waned. It was against this backdrop that the emergence of ASEAN+3 reflected the regional interest in re-grouping and constructing a framework for institutionalizing economic cooperation within the East Asian region (Webber 2001).

ASEAN+3 originally focussed on regional financial cooperation in response to the East Asian financial crisis (Terada 2003). However, the political circumstance that brought Japan, China and Korea together with the ASEAN group was more complex than the need to respond to the implications of the East Asian financial crisis. Disillusionment towards US domination of other global institutions was one factor (Ito and Narita 2004). Uncertainty in the relationship between Beijing and Washington in the wake of the Belgrade embassy bombing was another factor. To the East Asian powers, ASEAN+3 was a convenient insurance policy for East Asian dealings with Washington, and an expression of regional solidarity through socio-economic cooperation and interdependence. The concept of an emerging East Asian Community gathered momentum in the coming years, but the leadership contest between Japan and China gnawed at its core. Finally, by January 2002 in Singapore, Prime Minister Koizumi proposed extending the East Asian community to include cooperation beyond trade and financial issues to promote regional integration, with Australia and New Zealand among its members. In 2005, when the first East Asian Summit was convened, Australia, New Zealand and India were invited to participate in union with the ASEAN+3.

Growing bilateralism and a move towards sub-regional FTAs accompanied the emergence of the new East Asian regionalism after the East Asian financial crisis (Drysdale and Ishigaki 2002). Naturally, negotiating preferential or discriminatory trade arrangements was a strategy that ran counter to the principles upon which APEC was designed. It was a defensive, inward-looking form of regionalism that has still not comprehended the region as a whole. Thus, the insurance that GATT's non-discriminatory trade rule (Article 1) and APEC's initiative in steering the agreement of open trade in electronics and components through the WTO offered East Asia's newly emerging economies was threatened by new proposals and initiatives in East Asia which promoted bilateral FTAs of an explicitly discriminatory kind (Dent 2004). What has now emerged is a complex, and not very coherent, matrix composed of preferential bilateral narrowly conceived trade agreements around China, Japan, Korea and the ASEAN economies. There is as yet no comprehensive East Asian or Asia-Pacific economic arrangement that serves the interests of deeper regional integration through addressing behind-the-border reform issues although APEC, through Busan, Hanoi and Sydney identified this as a priority going forward. A crucial issue for East Asia's global agenda is to define a relationship between East Asian cooperation and integration that is complementary to trans-regional cooperation in Asia and the Pacific and the global agenda that is now being enunciated through the G-20 (Elek 2009).

Looking Forward

APEC has helped facilitate the search for a workable trade and economic diplomacy strategy in East Asia and the Pacific. Its policies of liberalization and reform organized around the principle of open regionalism (a strategy well-suited to the development objectives and diversity of the Asia Pacific region) have helped APEC, in its first twenty years, to establish an impressive record of achievement. From its beginnings, APEC has progressed to regular meetings of Asia-Pacific leaders in a forum where tensions can be calmed and political energies mobilized to deal with priority issues in each of its member states. In facilitating this dialogue, APEC has been able, for example, to synergize the three Chinese economies into a mutually productive economic framework. Moreover, it was able to influence the outcome of the Uruguay Round of trade negotiations and revealed its potential as a major coalition within the WTO. Its commitment to free trade and investment at Bogor has also seen the rise of a new mode in international trade liberalization.

APEC's political achievements are as important, if not more so, than its economic achievements. Its capacity to facilitate dialogue on important regional issues and ameliorate political tensions among the various Asia-Pacific powers (as between China and the United States, China and Japan, Australia and Indonesia) has been a crucial lynch-pin to its success. Thus, APEC's pre-eminence in the Asia-Pacific region persists despite the complementary evolution of East Asian regionalism following the East Asian economic crisis. Faced with the East Asian economic crisis, currency turmoil and macroeconomic instability, APEC extended its core agenda to encompass financial and other market strengthening programmes. APEC's position as the primary political meeting in the Asia-Pacific region remains unchallenged. Non-member countries like India are queuing up to be permitted a place at APEC's table once the embargo on new member economies expires at the Yokohama meeting in 2010.

The future of APEC depends on how the Asia-Pacific region moves to resolve the question of the relationship between the development of economic and political cooperation in East Asia and trans-Pacific cooperation with newly-developing South Asia. On the economic front, what China, Japan, ASEAN, Australia and the United States do in their approach to the negotiation of their new bilateral arrangements is crucial. Directing the negotiation of bilateral FTAs towards the progress of broad regional integration and towards East Asia's interests in an open global trading system should be a priority. The APEC conference in Chile took some steps towards this by adopting Best Practices for RTAs and FTAs. FTAs tinker at the edges of deeper integration: they do not address its core agenda which APEC has tentatively begun to define. Would a potential FTAAP, lead to much additional integration, even if it were ever negotiated? Elek (Chapter 1 in this volume) explains that even if APEC leaders agree to transform the process into a negotiating forum, the only trade deal available would be a lowest common denominator agreement which exempted border barriers on sensitive products from liberalization. On the now more important non-border barriers, a negotiation would not achieve anything that is not already being achieved in APEC working groups.

The Bogor Goals have also been a major component of APEC's work in the region, with the Busan roadmap, adopted at the 2005 conference confirming that APEC was well on the way to achieving the Bogor Goals. Furthermore, the Hanoi action plan, endorsed at the 2006 conference further identified specific actions and milestones along the road to complete realization of the Bogor Goals. The APEC conference in Sydney during 2007 saw APEC take on a new set of issues, with the member economies issuing a Declaration on Climate Change, Energy Security and Clean Development for the first time. By Lima, in 2008, solidarity in the face of the global financial crisis prompted the conference into committing to take all necessary measures to restore stability and growth to the region. The rhetoric can only, of course, be translated into action through active Asia-Pacific involvement in processes like the G-20 and linking those processes back to the region.

On the political front, Australian Prime Minister Rudd, has proposed the idea of an Asia-Pacific Community that aims at elevating the political and security dialogue among the major Asia-Pacific players. The Asia-Pacific Community idea needs to relate to APEC and East Asian structures if it is to be both accepted and to serve its underlying political-security purpose. It would be sensible for APEC to grab the initiative in taking this idea forward and host a small informal meeting (the idea is only worthwhile and practical if it limits dialogue to the major players) alongside the APEC Summit. Such a meeting would have to link to the East Asian Summit process by inviting India to join the meeting.

The change in the structure of regional economic and political power, with the rise of China and India, now recommends a step in that direction. If this initiative is not taken beforehand, APEC must seize the opportunity at Yokohama in 2010 to bring a more representative East and South Asian collection of economies to the APEC table and initiate its first explicit side-dialogue on political and security affairs. Though it cannot encompass all APEC's membership, or all the membership of EAS, a dialogue on political and security affairs needs to represent both as they are presently constituted, and in all probability is likely become a central driver of a truly Asia-Pacific Community that links to, is coordinated with, and draws on the base of all of the established trans-Pacific and East Asian arrangements.

Note

* The content of this essay draws, in part, from *Asia Pacific Economic Cooperation* (Vols. 1–5) edited by Peter Drysdale and Takashi Terada. London: Routledge, 2007). I wish to thank Ed Kus for his excellent research assistance in gathering and organizing the material on which the argument was developed. I alone am, of course, responsible for any inadequacies in its final form.

References

Aggarwal, V. K. "Building International institutions in Asia Pacific". *Asian Survey* 33, no. 11 (1993): 1029–42.

———. "APEC and Trade Liberalisation after Seattle: Transregionalism without a Cause". In *Reforming Economic Systems in Asia: A Comparative Analysis of China, Japan, South Korea, Malaysia and Thailand*, ed. M. Weber, pp. 149–78. Cheltenham, Elgar, 2001.

——— and C. E. Morrison. "APEC as an International Institution". In *APEC: Its Challenges and Tasks in the 21st Century*, ed. I. Yamazawa, pp. 298–324. New York: Routledge, 2000.

Ariff, M. "APEC and ASEAN: Complementing of Competing?". In *APEC: Challenges and Opportunities*, ed. Chia Siow Yue, pp. 151–74. Singapore: ISEAS, 1994.

Arndt, H. W. "PAFTA: An Australian Assessment". *Intereconomics*, vol. 10 (1967): 271–76.

Bergsten, C. F. "East Asian Regionalism: Towards a Tripartite World". *Economist* 356, no. 8179, (13 July 2000): 23–26.

Bonnor, J. "APEC's Contribution to Regional Security". In *The Role of Security and Economic Cooperation Structures in the Asia Pacific Region: Indonesian and Australian Views*, eds. H. Soesastro and A. Bergin, pp. 45–56. Jakarta: Centre for Strategic and International Studies, 1996.

Dent, C. M. "The Asia-Europe Meeting and Inter Regionalism: Toward a Theory of Multilateral Utility". *Asian Survey* 44, no. 2 (2004): 213–36.

Donowaki, M. "The Pacific Basin Community: A Japanese Overview". *Asia Pacific Community* 5 (winter 1982): 15–29.

Drysdale, P. "Policy Strategy". In *International Economic Pluralism: Economic Policy in East Asia and the Pacific*, pp. 256–61. Sydney: Allen & Unwin and Columbia University Press, 1988.

Drysdale, P. and Garnaut, R. "The Pacific: An Application of a General Theory of Economic Integration". In *Pacific Dynamism and the International Economic System*, eds C. F. Bergsten and M. Noland pp. 183–94, 212–23. Washington, DC: Institute of International Economics, 1993.

Drysdale, P. and K. Ishigaki. "New Issues in East Asian Economic Integration". In *East Asian Trade and Financial Integration: New Issues*, eds P. Drysdale and K. Ishigaki, pp. 3–12. Canberra, Asia Pacific Press, 2002.

Elek, A. "Trade Policy Options for the Asia Pacific Region in the 1990s". *American Economic Review* 82, no. 2 (1992): 1–7.

———. "Global Economic Integration". *The Indonesian Quarterly* 37, no. 1 (2009).

Funabashi, Y. *Asia Pacific Fusion: Japan's Role in APEC*. Washington, DC: Institute for International Economics, 1995.

Garnaut, R. *Open Regionalism and Trade Liberalisation: An Asia Pacific Contribution to*

the World Trade System. Sydney: Allen & Unwin, 1996.
Harris, S. "Policy Networks and Economic Cooperation: Policy Coordination in the Asia Pacific Region". *The Pacific Review* 7, no. 4 (1994): 381–95.
Higgott, R. "APEC: A Sceptical View". In *Pacific Cooperation: Building Economic and Security Regimes in the Asia Pacific Region*, eds. A. Mack and J. Ravenhill, Allen & Unwin, pp. 66–97. Sydney: St Leonards, 1994.
Ito, T. and K. Narita. "A Stocktake of Institutions for Regional Cooperation". In *Financial Governance in East Asia: Policy Dialogue, Surveillance and Cooperation*, eds. G. De Brouwer and Y. Wang, pp. 101–35. New York: RoutledgeCurzon, 2004.
Kahler, M. "Organizing the Pacific". In *Pacific-Asian Economic Policies and Regional Interdependence*, eds. R. Scalapino, S. Sato, J. Wanandi and S. Han, pp. 329–50. Berkeley, CA: Institute of East Asian Studies, 1988.
Petri, P. A. "The East Asian Trading Bloc: An Analytical History". In *Asia Pacific Regionlism: Readings in International Economic Relations*, eds. R. Garnaut and P. Drysdale, pp. 107–24. Sydney: Harper Educational, 1994.
Ravenhill, J. "APEC Adrift: Implications for Economic Regionalism in Asia and the Pacific". *The Pacific Review* 13, no. 2 (2000): 319–33.
Soesastro, H. "Pacific Economic Cooperation: The History of an Idea". In Asia Pacific Regionlism: Readings in *International Economic Relations*, eds. R. Garnaut and P. Drysdale, pp. 77–88. Sydney: Harper Educational, 1994.
———. "Towards and East Asia Regional Trading Arrangement". In *Reinventing ASEAN*, eds. S. C. Tay, H. Soesastro and J. P. Estanislao, pp. 226–42. Singapore: Institute of Southeast Asian Studies, 2001.
Tay, S. S. C. "ASEAN and East Asia: A new regionalism?". In *Reinventing ASEAN*, eds. S. C. Tay, H. Soesastro and J. P. Estanislao, pp. 206–25. Singapore: Institute of Southeast Asian Studies, 2001.
Terada, T. "Directional Leadership in Institution-Building: Japan's Approaches to ASEAN in the Establishment of PECC and APEC". *The Pacific Review* 14, no. 2 (2001): 196–220.
———. "Constructing an 'East Asian' Concept and Growing Regional Identity: From EAEC to ASEAN+3". *The Pacific Review* 16, no. 2 (2003): 251–77.
Webber, D. "Two Funerals and a Wedding? The Ups and Down of Regionalism in East Asia and Asia Pacific after the Asian Crisis". *The Pacific Review* 14, no. 3 (2001): 339–72.
Wesley, M. "APEC's Mid-life Crisis? The Rise and Fall of Early Voluntary Sectoral Liberalisation". *Pacific Affairs* 74, no. 2 (2001): 185–204.
Woolcott, R. A. *The Hot Seat*. Sydney: HarperCollins, 2003.
Yamazawa, I. "On Pacific Economic Integration". *The Economic Journal* 102, no. 415 (1992): 1519–29.

8. Mr Chen-Ku Koo, member of the Council on Economic Planning and Development of Chinese Taipei, arrives at the Ninoy Aquino International Airport, Manila, Philippines, to attend the APEC Summit in November 1996.
Photo courtesy of the APEC Secretariat.

9. The APEC Business Advisory Council (ABAC) provides feedback to the APEC process from a business perspective. In 1997, ABAC deliberated on the Manila Action Plan for APEC (MAPA) during the meeting in Vancouver, Canada. *Photo courtesy of the APEC Secretariat.*

10. First APEC Senior Officials Meeting held in Victoria, Canada, in January 1997. Senior Officials Meetings in the APEC process provide the groundwork to discuss issues at the end of each APEC year. *Photo courtesy of the APEC Secretariat.*

11. The APEC Business Advisory Council at its first plenary session of the fourth meeting in Shanghai, China, October 2001. *Photo courtesy of the APEC Secretariat.*

12. The APEC Australia 2007 Business Summit held in Sydney from 6 to 7 September continued to strengthen the bonds within the APEC region by bringing together business and economic leaders. The summit provided a platform and opportunity for building on the cooperation between businesses and governments within the Asia Pacific. *Photo courtesy of the APEC Secretariat.*

3

Four Adjectives Become a Noun: APEC The Future of Asia-Pacific Cooperation

Charles E. Morrison

The annual APEC Leaders Meeting, one of the largest regular gatherings of heads of state in the world, is frequently criticized in the media, which find it high on expense, ritual, and protocol, but low on concrete achievements. For example, *The Economist*, following the 2007 Sydney meeting, wrote a scathing assessment describing APEC as a stale joke: "It is not just that APEC has no obvious function. It is worse than that: it actually has a pernicious effect. Its very existence creates the illusion that something is being done, and so weakens other efforts to reach meaningful agreements on, for example, climate change and trade."[1] Other more dispassionate assessments of APEC, particularly in its second decade, have also been sceptical. Writing shortly after the association's tenth anniversary, John Ravenhill found APEC "adrift".[2] Allan Gyngell and Malcolm Cook contended in 2005 that APEC was "balanced on the brink of terminal irrelevance".[3] More recently, the Pacific Economic Cooperation Council's annual surveys of regional business, government, and academic élites found that even these adherents of Asia-Pacific cooperation demonstrate considerable dissatisfaction with the performance of Asia-Pacific regional institutions, including APEC.[4]

If achieving concrete, near-term policy outcomes should be the measure of APEC's success, the institution would surely come up far short. But this misses the main point. For those who foresaw that the Asia-Pacific region was rapidly replacing the trans-Atlantic region as the core area of global growth and governance, APEC was and remains an essential institution, bringing the leading economies on both sides of the Pacific together in a common forum and cooperative, on-going process. It is the most significant multilateral connection across the Pacific, and its very existence softens the impact of (and thus helps to flourish) the more geographically restricted regionalisms in both East Asia and the Americas.

Multinational and intergovernmental institutions — from the United Nations to the smallest organization — begin with dreams, but are established through compromises among the sovereign states that create them. In APEC's case, there was opposition in the initial meeting in 1989 to anything that would suggest an on-going organization. The host Australian Foreign Minister Gareth Evans famously described the new "Asia-Pacific Economic Cooperation" as "four adjectives in search of a noun" in that there was no final word such as forum, council, or community to describe what the enterprise was intended to be. In two decades, APEC never acquired the noun, but it was institutionalized and the acronym itself became the noun. It has also been a part and parcel of a signification transformation in the international life of the Asia-Pacific region.

It is important to recall what the Asia-Pacific region was like before APEC was created, and to try to imagine what the region might look like today without it. Prior to APEC's creation, there was no venue for the leaders of the largest powers — China, Japan, and the United States — to meet on a regular basis. Territorial and other issues were often left to fester, and national economic policies were frequently conducted on a "beggar thy neighbour" basis with no scope for international review.[5] Regional cooperation was either non-existent, limited to sub-regional institutions, or took place in highly specialized arenas, with no sense of a broad and converging regional agenda. Regional engagement with global issues was sporadic and uncoordinated, even at the rhetorical level. Without an APEC to connect across the Pacific, there undoubtedly would have been more suspicion and tensions created over the establishment of the North American Free Trade Area and the later establishment of East Asian regional cooperation mechanisms. APEC helped consolidate a norm of economic "openness", on which many of the region's interdependent economies depend. The pledges of adherence to this norm remain highly relevant in the contemporary economic crisis, all the more so that the impulses towards protectionism remain and find occasional expression.

This, of course, is not to say that APEC has resolved all of these problems, but it certainly does help provide an atmosphere that encourages the resolution of disputes, the maintenance of open economic systems, and expectations of cooperation on major issues. It has also fostered Asia-Pacific "communities" of individuals, mostly within bureaucracies but also in some academic and business circles, who are personally comfortable with one another, better understand the interests and political dynamics of their counterparts' societies, increasingly speak and think in similar policy terms, and are generally more prepared to engage in international cooperation. It is safe to say that were there no APEC, there would be a greater sense of insecurity among the Asia-Pacific nations, less convergence of national actions, more unchecked protectionist pressures, and, most certainly, urgent calls to create an intergovernmental Asia-Pacific organization.

In the longer run, success for APEC will not be measured against whether it has achieved its 1994 Bogor trade and investment goal or some similar bureaucratic target. Nor will it be whether APEC has developed a significant organizational capability or even itself survives as an institution. APEC's significance will lie in whether it is widely perceived to have had a transformative impact on prospects for international order in the Asia-Pacific region and globally, and whether it leads to something more.

Despite the changes associated with the APEC process, APEC relevance is being tested. It is important to emphasize the word "process", since above all APEC is about relationship and norm building among its member economies. It has never had serious rule-making and negotiating functions, and the slow, incremental growth of its organizational structure has come against the resistance of those who remain reluctant to "institutionalize" it. Processes, however, are continuous, have purpose, and eventually must lead to something more. APEC and other multilateral institutions in the Asia-Pacific region face still greater challenges ahead that will require some fundamental rethinking. This chapter evaluates some of the limitations and obstacles APEC confronts and concludes with suggestions about how the architecture of Asia-Pacific cooperation might be enhanced.

An Improbable Region

The notion of a regional community combines in some way physical geography and human imagination. Clearly, a "region" requires some element of geographical propinquity. The newly emerging "BRICs", consisting of Brazil, Russia, India, and China, for example, may share some similarities in their size, stage of economic development, and presumed continuing high growth trajectories, but they are not regarded as a region. Despite geographical realities, the human construction of regions can change. Two thousand years ago, the lands surrounding the Mediterranean were clearly part of a geographic, economic, and political region; in fact, the Mediterranean was an internal sea and indispensable transportation connector within the interdependent Roman Empire. But from the time of the Muslim conquest of northern Africa until today, it has more often been viewed as a boundary than a bridge on both its southern and northern shores.

The vast Pacific Ocean, comprising half of the surface area of the globe, was also historically considered a barrier.[6] The notion that the nations around its rim are in some way geographically connected, constitute a region, and may even form a potential Asia-Pacific "community" requires a enormous leap of imagination. Thus a Pacific definition of an Asia-Pacific "region" clearly much owes more to human construction than natural geography.[7] By the standards of any more conventionally defined region, the now 21 members of APEC, comprising parts or the whole of four continents, are widely scattered and enormously divergent in economic and political systems, culture and history. This matters in explaining why APEC can achieve so little in concrete terms; it is more like the United Nations than it is like a regional group closely knit by geography, culture, and shared interests.

Re-imagining the rim as a community was more a political idea than an economic one. The dramatic growth of economic interdependence since the 1960s provided a strong rationale for a Pacific-based organization. By the 1980s, the trade across the Pacific was double that across the Atlantic. But more importantly, APEC's establishment coincided with the end of the Cold War and the uncertainty about the future of the regional and international system. This political upheaval both removed constraints and provided incentives. APEC was formed as a new piece of multilateral architecture spanning the Pacific at a time when the future of some of the older elements (including bilateral alliances and the anti-Soviet based Sino-American entente) was in doubt.

This was background music, however, and soon taken for granted. In the 1990s, however, APEC was an untried vehicle and it seemed alive with possibilities. Nations lined at the door, hoping for admission. The four-year-old APEC was given a huge boost with the convening of the Leaders Meeting in 1993, followed by the adoption of free trade in the region goal at the second Leaders Meeting in Bogor in 1994. The process seemed to be gaining further momentum with the Osaka Action Agenda in 1995 and the Manila Plan of Action in 1996. But when it became time for real "action", as opposed to talking about and planning for it, APEC was poorly equipped because it simply had not been designed for this purpose. Moreover, the possibilities for action had been narrowed by some of the decisions-taking during this earlier period of high hubris: the widening of the institution, the priority placed on free trade in Bogor, and the progressive clogging of the agenda with virtually each meeting.

The Widening of APEC

Like many multilateral regional institutions, APEC widened before it could be deepened. All of this widening occurred during the first decade when APEC's membership expanded in increments from 12 founding member countries, to 15 "member economies", and from there to 18 by 1994, and 21 in 1998. The group then wisely put a hold on membership that has continued for a decade. This expansion enormously increased the diversity of the group. Even the original twelve founders could hardly be considered "like-minded", but they were more alike than the later additions. The first accretion — the People's Republic of China, "Chinese Taipei", and Hong Kong — was integrally linked to the increasingly interdependent trans-Pacific economy. This certainly made sense in terms of the declared focus of the organization, but greatly increased the association's political heterogeneity. It also created problems in further institutional development, especially after the APEC Leaders Meeting was established in 1993, as China refused to allow Taiwan to be admitted at the leader level and inhibited the otherwise quite natural evolution of APEC towards a more comprehensive agenda, including political and security affairs, a path more easily taken by ASEAN.

The additions after 1991 were less weighty, but expanded the institution well beyond its original core area, and added to growing diversity. These additions owed less to any vision of Asia-Pacific, its multilateral architecture, or APEC's stated economic objectives, than they did to other foreign policy goals of the sponsors of the new members. This was particularly true of the United States, which pushed the inclusion of the Russian Federation and Latin American members.

Widening ahead of deepening always creates action problems, although APEC might not have deepened much anyway. Most of the post-1991 members have played relatively minor roles in the institution, whose basic tone remains set by the first 15. However, they add to the numbers, and each has a claim to taking a year's turn at hosting and institutional leadership. The new members have largely been seen by the original sponsors as more focused on development and domestic prestige goals and less on issues of interdependence and regional and global order. Informally, APEC insiders in the advanced countries refer to strong and weak hosts and are delighted, for example, by the happenstance of back-to-back hosting of Singapore (2009), Japan (2010), and the United States (2011), providing a three-year stretch of leadership by advanced, founding members. Outside this stretch, during the decade from 2002 through 2012, nearly half of the hosting is provided by the newer members.

The Trade Agenda

While this essay has situated APEC's creation principally in the international political environment, many others would privilege economic drivers. As so often with the creation of institutions, there was no single vision, but multiple visions that could be served by the same institution. One, which has a history going back into the 1960s, was a "free trade" vision. This vision gained prominence in the early 1990s, when APEC established a temporary "Eminent Persons Group" (EPG) under the chairmanship of C. Fred Bergsten and including other prominent trade economists. The EPG was highly

13. *Above*: The APEC CEO Summit meeting in Shanghai, China, in October 2001, discussed the issue: "New Century, New Economy: Developing in the Globalizing World". *Photo courtesy of the APEC Secretariat.*

14. *Right*: Singapore Prime Minister Goh Chok Tong chatting with Malaysian Prime Minister Mahathir, and Chief Executive of Hong Kong, China, Tung Chee Hwa, at the APEC Economic Leaders' Meeting, Shanghai International Convention Centre in October 2001. *Photo courtesy of the APEC Secretariat.*

15. APEC Economic Leaders' Meeting, Los Cabos, Mexico 2002. In that year, leaders adopted a Trade Facilitation Action Plan among other matters and also provided APEC's second Counter-Terrorism Statement, along with the adoption of the Secure Trade in the APEC Region (STAR) initiative. *Photo courtesy of the APEC Secretariat.*

16. APEC Health Ministers from the various member economies meeting on 28 June 2003, to discuss the Severe Acute Respiratory Syndrome (SARS) in Bangkok, Thailand. *Photo courtesy of the APEC Secretariat.*

17. Dr Surakiart Sathirathai, Thai Foreign Minister, delivering the Opening Remarks at the First APEC SOM in Chiang Rai, Thailand, on 20 February 2003. *Photo courtesy of the APEC Secretariat.*

18. The APEC SOMs were an important part of the APEC process. In May 2003, at Khon Kaen, Thailand, officials deliberated on the promotion of structural reform related to liberalization and facilitation of trade and investment activities for APEC member economies. *Photo courtesy of the APEC Secretariat.*

19. The APEC Meeting of Ministers Responsible for Trade which was held in Khon Kaen, Thailand, from 1 to 3 June 2003. In this meeting, APEC agreed to re-energize the Doha Development Agenda negotiations. *Photo courtesy of the APEC Secretariat.*

20. Dr Tej Bunnag, providing the Concluding Remarks at the APEC 2003 SOM Chair APEC/IFI Roundtable Discussion on Economic and Technical Cooperation in Phuket, Thailand, 22 to 23 August 2003. *Photo courtesy of the APEC Secretariat.*

influential in pushing APEC towards a trade and investment focus, which was crystallized in the APEC Leaders 1994 Bogor Declaration setting out a long-term goal of "free and open trade and investment in the Asia-Pacific", to be achieved for developed economies by 2010 and for the group as a whole by 2020.

Bogor provided a focal point for an APEC agenda and established a target for criticism when the trade agenda stalled. APEC now had a goal, but it was ill-defined and there was no solid mechanism for achieving it. APEC developed an approach based on "concerted voluntary liberalization" formulated in individual and collective action plans, but this depended upon the will of the individual members in undertaking unilateral liberalization. This flew in the face of the established rule-making system and reciprocity through the General Agreement on Tariffs and Trade (GATT) and then the World Trade Organization (WTO), which also privileged at least the formal saving of "trade concessions" as bargaining chips with other parties in global negotiating rounds.

When the United States sought to test APEC's potential as a negotiating institution by pushing a set of sectoral liberalizations, this floundered both because of the Asian economic crisis and Asian political constraints, especially in Northeast Asia on agriculture. The Doha Round added to the premium for saving concessions. With the failure of Early Voluntary Sectoral Liberalization, the emphasis was sensibly shifted towards trade facilitation. On this, APEC claimed victories, but it is difficult to discern how much the lowering of business transaction costs owes to APEC as opposed to other factors. APEC also began to develop standards (model measures) for the proliferating free trade agreements in the area (a norm-setting exercise) and explore linking these over the longer-term into a Free Trade Agreement of Asia and the Pacific (FTAAP). Again, however, even if the political will were there for the establishment of an FTAAP, the necessary negotiating mechanism is lacking.[8]

APEC's most important contribution in trade liberalization may be very difficult to quantify and take credit for. As a result of APEC's trade agenda and the need to advance and defend the trade policies of member economies through their Individual Action Plans and a peer review process, national bureaucracies, particularly in developing countries, learn more about and hopefully better implement, existing trade obligations. In this sense, APEC may be less "WTO-plus" in negotiating new liberalizing measures than in helping to deepen the WTO process through stronger adherence to existing disciplines. It is also said that for China and Vietnam, and possibly for Russia, a great deal of learning about the WTO occurred through earlier engagement in APEC trade activities.

Bureaucratic Momentum

A third problem was the clogging of the APEC agenda, which has contributed to a general lack of flexibility in addressing emerging issues. APEC's central secretariat in Singapore is small and primarily limited to logistic support for the processes that engage national bureaucracies. But there has been a proliferation of ministerial meetings, committees and working groups, as well as a host of on-going initiatives. These have sometimes derived from the ephemeral emphasis that individual economies placed on issues during their year of leadership, leaving behind a residue of expectations and perhaps a working group but lacking continuous political support. The proliferation may have the advantage of building Asia-Pacific awareness in the bureaucracies beyond those in foreign affairs, trade, and economic ministries with more obvious international interests. The danger is that they are too fragmented to have much significance and suck organizational oxygen from addressing more critical emerging issues.

When new challenges arise, they may not get much initial attention unless covered by a pre-existing agenda, particularly if it is a long time until the next Leaders or Ministerial meeting. On 26 December 2004, a quarter of a million citizens of APEC economies vanished in a tsunami, with no mention, not even condolences, appearing on the APEC official website for weeks.

APEC's most spectacular response failure came in the Asian economic crisis of 1997–98, when the organization — although focused on economic issues of interdependence — seemed institutionally ill-equipped to act. In the years afterwards, the affected economies naturally reacted by developing national responses (such as building foreign exchange reserves) and establishing or strengthening other multilateral configurations, especially Asian-only institutions. Ten years later in 2007–09, when the world faced another economic crisis, APEC was still lethargic. Indeed, the crisis was a global one, and required global responses, but APEC might have been a structure through which some consultation and exercise of global leadership could have taken place. But its November 2008 Lima Ministerial Meeting in Lima was dominated by the existing agenda.

There have been other instances, however, where APEC has responded to serious immediate challenges. In 1999, the Ministers and Leaders could not ignore the political and human rights tragedy that came to a head in East Timor just as they were convening in Auckland. In Shanghai in 2001, two months after the 9/11 terrorist attacks on the United States, the APEC Leaders focused on terrorism. Both instances, however, also show the limitations of APEC in dealing directly with political-security issues. The East Timor issue had to be addressed on the side of the formal APEC meetings, and APEC's foray into security after 2001 brought heavy resistance and was carefully circumscribed.

Challenges for APEC at Twenty Years

For those who had hoped that APEC would develop into a region-wide free trade area or become an OECD of the Pacific, it has probably performed significantly below expectations. For those who see APEC principally as a venue for promoting political, cultural, and personal connections across the Pacific and developing norms, the institution looks much better. APEC's annual, back-to-back Ministerial and Leaders Meetings are huge gatherings of several thousand political, bureaucratic, and business leaders, a little more like an international fair or a UN General Assembly meeting than the working meeting of a regional cooperation group. As for the real work, multilateralism takes second fiddle to bilateralism. Bilateral meetings dominate leader and ministerial schedules, as well as those of many business people who come to see individual government leaders in small group meetings. Even the "CEO Summit" is essentially a series of bilateral business encounters with leaders. In this way, APEC has become a very efficient, high-level meeting venue, sometimes facetiously described as a "dating service" for leaders. As an example, George H. Bush's last trip to Asia as president covered 25,000 miles, in the course of which he met only four counterparts. His son was able to see 18 counterparts annually in a single venue.

Because of APEC's valuable meeting function and because it is the only general cooperation institution bridging the Pacific, there is no significant threat to its survival. No new Chinese, Japanese, Indonesian, or American leader, much less the leader of one of the smaller Asia-Pacific economies, is likely to question whether he or she needs to attend the APEC Leaders Meeting. For Asian leaders, there are now several other opportunities to meet with Asian counterparts, but few or none to see their American ones. The U.S. President also has other opportunities to see the leaders of larger Asian nations in multilateral settings (e.g., at the G-8 or more recently at the G-20), but not the large group he meets at APEC.

But this does not mean that APEC will or should be allowed to remain the way it is. From a political and public perspective, the biggest challenge for APEC will not be in meeting goals set in the past or failing to have a robust enough regional integration agenda. Rather it lies in whether APEC is adequately performing the functions required of multilateral cooperation in the Asia-Pacific region in the 21st century. While there are those who are quite content with the incremental fine-tuning of the current institutions, others believe there needs to be a top to bottom review of architecture and quite possibly some fundamental change. Prime Minister Kevin Rudd of Australia has been the most prominent contemporary political leader to challenge the adequacy of the current architecture.[9]

The Future of Asia-Pacific Architecture

The major global changes in the past two decades have made it increasingly clear that the trans-Pacific region will be the central focal point of the global system. This means that the region requires both robust internal mechanisms for addressing regional issues and effective means of consulting and providing leadership on global issues. This raises three key areas where the current regional architecture, including APEC, comes up short. The first is about the coverage of regional security. The second relates to the extent to which the region consults on global issues, and third concerns rapid responses to new challenges.

Clearly, the biggest lacuna in the architecture lies in the political-security realm. The premier trans-Pacific security dialogue, the ASEAN Regional Forum (ARF), does not operate at the leaders' level. APEC does, but for the reasons relating to Taiwan already discussed, political-security issues for the most part enter indirectly, through informal meetings or the bilateral side meetings. Thus they cannot be easily or naturally addressed, nor can discussions be prepared through background material collected or analysed by the APEC secretariat. The United States sought to bring security into APEC as early as 1995, and more forcefully between 2001 and 2003, but was rebuffed.

One solution often suggested is for the United States to join the East Asian Summit (EAS), which does not include Taiwan and thus does not face the same set of constraints. The EAS also excludes the Latin American nations which have a limited interest in Asia-Pacific political and security issues. But despite some advantages to this new summit configuration, this does not seem very likely unless the EAS were restructured to be an equal partnership among its members rather than privileging one group as drivers and agenda-setters. And while not including Taiwan, EAS does include Myanmar, which has increasingly become a pariah nation. Finally, should the EAS become a venue for addressing political-security issues, there is the question of why leaders, especially the president of the United States, would want to continue to attend a second Asia-Pacific meeting on economic issues. For these reasons, it may seem more logical to find some way to allow the APEC Leaders Meeting, as large as it, to be renamed and given a separate identity from APEC, so that it can deal directly with political-security issues. This would not mean that the economic issues discussed in APEC would not come to them for final review. It would simply mean that political-security issues could also be addressed because the new, separate leaders' meeting would not include "economies" that are not generally recognized as sovereign state actors.

Even as Asia-Pacific nations need to adjust their own relationships to meet changing power relationships among them, they also need to adjust their relationships with the rest of the world to reflect the region's relative rise and increased capabilities to provide global public goods. Even in the economic arena, however, and despite ritualistic statements in support of WTO processes with each APEC Ministers and Leaders Meeting, APEC does not truly have a global outlook. This could be enhanced by greater efforts to address global issues in work programmes and retreats, backed by appropriate analytical capabilities. The latter need not be the internal product of some OECD-type structure, but drawn from think-tank networks within and outside the governments.

Rapid response capacities are closely related and require similar support. APEC need not be a principal venue for discussion of every regional and global issue, but it should have a secretariat that monitors such issues and considers whether and how APEC should respond with the understanding that for institutional development, every crisis is indeed a potential opportunity.

Needed: New Asia-Pacific Champions

Probably the most important requirement for a new wind of broad Asia-Pacific cooperation would be to find national champions for the regional process. These have been sadly lacking recently, but in the early years of APEC, the champions came mainly from Australia and Japan, who pulled along the more reluctant — some of the ASEAN countries and the United States. For both countries — allies of the United States and with strong interests in stronger connections with Asian neighbours — APEC neatly combined two major foreign policy interests, and avoided having to make choices. But both lost some interest. Australia lacks systemic weight, and the Howard government placed priority on its American connection. More recently, Rudd has sought to re-establish Australia as a source of regional cooperation ideas. In Japan's case, there was a strong shift towards Asian regionalism, in part in competition with China. Japan's potential leadership has been undercut by frequent changes in political leadership. The exception was Junichiro Koizumi's prime ministership between 2001 and 2006, but a period in which Sino-Japanese relations sharply deteriorated because of Koizumi's trips to the controversial Yasukuni Shrine, undermining Japan's effectiveness as a potential regional leader.

The United States has systemic weight and should have a strong interest in the further development of Asia-Pacific regional cooperation, now more than ever before. The United States needs East Asian partners to accomplish almost any foreign policy goal, and its engagement with them should be multilateral as well as bilateral. But the United States has rarely been the champion that its interests suggest it should be. The George H. Bush administration was initially skeptical, largely supporting APEC as a means to head off East Asian proposals. The Bill Clinton Administration was initially highly supportive, and made a major contribution by convening the first Leaders Meeting. But it found APEC's process orientation at conflict with its own outcome rhetoric, and its interest was not sustained. As mentioned, the George W. Bush administration has appreciated APEC as a venue for meeting other leaders, and Bush attended every APEC Leaders Meeting during his tenure. His first international travel after 9/11 was for APEC, as was his last travel as president. But the interest was mostly reactive, peaking at the time of the meetings and waning otherwise, with little attention given to how APEC might strategically fit into a broad U.S. foreign or Asia-Pacific policy framework.

The Barack Obama Administration has yet to formulate an Asia-Pacific or APEC strategy. The new administration already has multiple foreign and domestic initiatives. However, it clearly appreciates the value of multilateral diplomacy and there are certainly indications that it appreciates the weight of Asia in global affairs. Obama will be making his first APEC trip to Singapore in November 2009, and this is bound to force thinking about the broad outlines of Asia-Pacific policy on the part of a president whose formative international experience was in Southeast Asia. The new American leadership, combined with a set of changing international relations dynamics that encourage multilateralism in U.S. policy, may yet be the best hope for new wind in the sails of the noun "APEC" and trans-Pacific regional cooperation.

Notes

1. *The Economist*, "APEC — A Pretty Empty Chatter," 12 September 2007.
2. John Ravenhill, *APEC and the Construction of Pacific Rim Regionalism* (Cambridge University Press, 2001), chapter 5.
3. Allen Gyngell and Malcolm Cook, "How to Save APEC", Policy Brief, *Lowy Institute for International Policy*, October 2005, p. 4.
4. Pacific Economic Cooperation Council, *The State of the Region: 2007–2008* (PECC 2007), p. 26.
5. See Lawrence B. Krause, "The Pacific Basin and Economic Regionalism," in Joint Economic Committee, U.S. Congress, *Pacific Region Interdependencies: A Compendium of Papers*, 15 June 1981, pp. 11–16.
6. Ravenhill, pp. 42–43.
7. For example, in a book written in 1989 just before the establishment of APEC, Normal D. Palmer refers to its predecessor non-governmental and business organizations (the Pacific Economic Cooperation Council and the Pacific Basin Economic Council) as "interregional organizations". *The New Regionalism in Asia and the Pacific* (Lexington Books, 1991), chapter 8.
8. On the FTAAP, see Charles E. Morrison and Eduardo Pedrosa, eds., *An APEC Trade Agenda? The Political Economy of a Free Trade Area of the Asia-Pacific* (Singapore: Institute of Southeast Asian Studies, 2007).
9. Kevin Rudd, "Keynote Address". The 8th IISS Asian Security Summit, The Shangri-La Dialogue, Singapore, 29 May 2009.

21. APEC Economic Leaders' Meeting, Osaka, Japan, November 1995. APEC adopts the Osaka Action Plan which provided a framework for meeting the Bogor Goals. *Photo courtesy of the APEC Secretariat.*

4

APEC's Eye on the Prize: Participants, Modality, and Confidence-Building

Man-jung Mignonne Chan

In commemoration of those who have been treading through the APEC paths with devotion to a better future during the past two decades, this chapter assesses APEC's future prospects by highlighting the past aspirations as well as unexpected setbacks. The scope of this chapter will mainly focus on the following three dimensions that are manifested in some personality theory, philosophical underpinning, organizational theory, system theory, and management theory:

(1) *Participants*: Distinction will be made between liberal/idealists, realists, and constructivists and their respective impacts on unilateralism, multilateralism, and constructivism.
(2) *Modality*: The APEC modus operandi will be explored by contrasting two key conceptualizing principles, namely "concerted unilateralism" vis-à-vis "competitive liberalization".
(3) *APEC as an Institution in the Geopolitical Dynamics*: The structure and functions of APEC as an institution, particularly in the context of geopolitical dynamics, such as the challenge of WTO negotiations, the Asian financial crisis, and the 9/11 terrorists attack on the World Trade Center at New York City in 2001.

APEC Participants: Various Levels of Expectation, Satisfaction, Trust, and Comfort

In the assessment of APEC achievements and setbacks, APEC participants as a significant factor cannot be underestimated. For the sake of illustration, three contrasting types of people stand out in the APEC corridors: one bears the liberal/idealist's temperament, another wears the realist's jacket, by choice or at others' command, and still another strives to be the constructivist in pursuit of common interests. Many sit or swing somewhere in between these three typologies[1] with issue-specific and time-bound circumstances.

The liberal/idealists attend APEC meetings in good faith. They believe that cooperation is possible, and see *laws* as one of the major instruments for framing and maintaining good order in the international system. The realists believe in the roles of *deterrence* and *balance of power* in global governance more than international organizations per se, and consider APEC as a useful locus for function-specific targets, and with the aspiration to manoeuvre policy directions, stage power plays, and at times bully when timely, or impose isolation against others where necessary. The realists also emphasize interest calculation, high-flying scorecards, and outcome-oriented deliverables within a specific time-frames.

The constructivists maintain that the behaviours of individuals, states, and other actors are shaped by shared beliefs, socially constructed rules, and cultural practices. The constructivists believe that human beings are capable of changing the world by changing ideas, and hence the determination to show how identities and interests of actors are "socially constructed". Constructivists see institutional designs as "rational, negotiated responses to the problems international actors face".[2] Constructivists criticize those who see sovereignty as unchanging and illustrate various transformations in their understanding of sovereignty since Westphalia, influenced by both states and non-state actors.[3] International organizations may serve as agents of social construction, and as norm entrepreneurs. The constructivists stress harmonious process, consensus building, and open-ended outcomes of a convergent or invariant nature in a given time. The constructivists attend APEC with the aspiration to witness an ideal-type regional organization, capable of orchestrating policy decisions, enforcing policy implementation, and achieving common good for the APEC community.

Within each of the three camps — liberal/idealist, realist, and constructivist camps — there are inclinations towards unilateral or multilateral approaches in the scheme of things in APEC. In the liberal/idealist camp, there are unilateralism-inclined-idealists and multilateralism-inclined-idealists. The former uphold self-generated exemplary and self-exercised restraint, whereas the latter stress the importance of "best practice" as the means to achieving common good.

In the realist camp, there are unilateralism-inclined-realists and multilateralism-inclined-realists. The former tend to toy with self-centred calculations on national interests or stage self-righteous or irrevocable one-off initiatives. The latter values balance of power, and aims at maximal scoring with carrot-and-stick manoeuvring.

In the constructivist camp, there are also unilateralism-inclined-constructivists and multilateralism-inclined-constructivists. The former stress active and self-disciplined participation in dialogues, whereas the latter value consensus-building, cherish wider scope of stakeholders' participation and promote collective will and collaborative actions.

Inevitably, APEC insiders as well as outsiders-looking-in have various perspectives on APEC's scorecards, given the diverse aptitudes and expectations that meet their various appetites. Take for instance the IAP (Individual Action Plan) peer review sessions, and the negotiations on EVSL (Early Voluntary Sectoral Liberalization) during 1996–97. One can easily observe some phenomenal dynamics at play. Some left these APEC gatherings with a certain dose of satisfaction or a strong sense of achievement, some could not hide their frustration and dismay, still others urged for APEC reform with strong missionary passion. Some are comfortable with APEC's endowments of voluntarism, flexibility, and mutual benefits, others grew to be rather impatient about the pace of change within APEC, anxious about converting APEC into an otherwise more rule-binding, enforceable, and perhaps WTO-like architecture.

The portfolio of APEC participants is the core component for the APEC process. It not only affects the project initiatives, stakeholders' participation eligibility, and membership expansion, but also determines institutional identity, level of confidence, and future outlook of APEC.

Ideally, APEC constructivists will carry on the torch of those who have run their course earlier, and sustain the APEC momentum in line with the earlier founders and participants. A constructivist is characterized by realist idealism and is committed to consensus building. All members are entitled to address their issues of concern, and deserve to be heard. The APEC sense of community would be worthy of its substance if it is geared more towards constructivism. Over the years, we see variations in the aptitudes of the movers and shapers of the APEC issue agenda, including Chairs of Committees and Lead Shepherds of Working Groups, Senior Officials, Ministers, and Leaders. Their respective orientations and the participating modes are determining factors upon which the success or failure of initiatives hinges, and the goodwill spreads or ill faith ferments.

APEC over time has also enhanced its partnership with other stakeholders, such as business, academia, and civil society. Inclusion of constructive stakeholders should be in order as the confidence-building process in the past two decades should have generated some mutual learning, maturity, and voluntary initiatives. MOUs, guidelines and the like could be in due course revisited as a gesture of goodwill and a symbol of maturity. It would also serve as an

FIGURE 4.1
APEC Participants: Faith, Inclination, and Project Preference

	Unilateralism	*Multilateralism*	*Constructivism (consensus-building)*
Liberal/Idealists	⋆ IAP ⋆ self-generated exemplary; ⋆ self-exercised restraints	⋆ CAP ⋆ Best practice ⋆ Model guidelines	⋆ Concerted unilaterialism ⋆ Peer review
Realists	⋆ EVSL ⋆ Financial crisis management; ⋆ self-centered interests; ⋆ self-righteous initiatives	⋆ ITA ⋆ FTAAP ⋆ Dispute resolution; ⋆ balance of power; ⋆ carrots-and-sticks	⋆ Competitive liberalization ⋆ Rule-based reform;
Constructivists (realistic idealism)	⋆ active, self-disciplined participation in dialogues;	⋆ wider scope of stakeholders' participation; ⋆ "21-X" ⋆ Path-finder	⋆ Bogor Goals; ⋆ current issues of concern; ⋆ Contingency management on issues of concerns

inspiring exemplary for promoting peace and prosperity in the region.

APEC's Modality: Concerted Unilateralism vis-à-vis Competitive Liberalization?

Having made the distinction between participants' categories, let us examine the two contrasting approaches: the liberal/idealists' "concerted unilateralism" and the realists' "competitive liberalization".

1. Concerted Unilateralism:[4] Modus Operandi in Good Faith?

The term "concerted unilateralism" implies a "unity of the opposite" and assumes that collective-consensus and unilateral action could and should co-exist in harmony. The rationale for reconciling the seemingly contradictory term is most evident in APEC's modus operandi on the basis of consensus and with explicit recognition of the diversity among member economies, underlined in the APEC Canberra Ministerial Statement in November 1989:

- Cooperation should recognize the diversity of the region, including differing social and economic systems and current levels of development;
- Cooperation should involve a commitment to open dialogue and

consensus, with equal respect for the views of all participants.

In the early years, there had been formal and informal debates on what constitutes "consensus". Some innovative approaches such as "general consensus", "flexible consensus", "21-X", or the "Pathfinder" were entertained.

The ASEAN member economies proclaimed their joint stance in participating in the APEC process at the ASEAN Ministerial Meeting in 1990 with the Kuching Consensus:

- An enhanced APEC should be based on principles of equality, equity, and mutual benefit, taking fully into account the differences in stages of economic development and socio-political systems among the member economies in the region;
- APEC should provide a consultative forum on economic issues and should not lead to the adoption of mandatory directives for any participant to undertake or implement.

APEC's modus operandi for achieving the Bogor Goals entail the notion of "*concerted unilateralism*". On the one hand, the Collective Action Plans (CAPs) within the various APEC fora provide benchmarks for guiding progress on specific issue areas; on the other hand, the Individual Action Plans (IAPs) prepared by each member economy serve as engines for progress, in light of the CAPs and on a voluntary and non-binding basis, towards the Bogor Goals. Nevertheless, IAPs are not confined to the scope of CAPs, as many economies took unilateral approaches which transcended beyond the consensus approach of the CAPs. These *IAPs could serve as catalysts or pathfinders* for cheering APEC partners along with a sense of community.

The CAPs had their share of glory when the Information Technology Agreement (ITA) was initiated in 1996, and was carried both in APEC and then in the WTO. However, CAPs also have their constraints in that they could run in vain due to: (1) lack of consensus; (2) lack of leadership for an innovative approach to consensus building; (3) lack of concrete measurable targets after general principles are established; (4) lack of concerted efforts in capacity building, or (5) lack of mapping out implementation timeframes. The failed attempt of the Early Voluntary Sectoral Liberalization (EVSL) in 1997, for instance, is a case in point. Few would perhaps take pains to recall the ill-fated, EVSL-turned-ATI (Advanced Tariff Initiative) in disguise that was launched at the WTO. The ATI did not withstand the calculated manoeuvring by a few: it was "postponed indefinitely" on the WTO platform, as the APEC "defectors" had no stomach to serve as "champions" or "endorsers" for the aborted APEC initiative.

IAP Review Process

Appropriate peer pressure could instill a sense of community, which is essential to achieve economic growth and social welfare across the Asia-Pacific region with mutual respect and mutual benefits. The IAP Peer Review Process, endorsed by APEC Ministers in 2001 and enhanced by other revised directives, is aimed at increasing the rigour of the peer review mechanism and encouraging member economies to make greater progress in achieving the Bogor Goals. It is therefore not adversarial; rather, it is an interactive process that will ultimately result in a mutual learning experience for all APEC members and individuals involved.

The approach of concerted unilateral liberalization based on the premise that liberalization is beneficial to those who embrace it, and thus is pursued for their own good. However, the non-binding, voluntary, and therefore seemingly non-contestable, non-sanctionable nature of the APEC approach has turned controversial, explicitly or implicitly, mainly with growing impatience over the slow pace of progress in pursuit of the Bogor Goals, and further intensified by frustration due to the lack of effective instruments to turn things around. This was particularly acute with the advent of the Asian Financial Crisis of 1997–98 when finger-pointing and mutual distrust were at play. This is mainly due to the fact that the idea of creating an Asian Monetary Fund was strongly opposed by the U.S.

2. Concerted Unilateralism: An Ill-Fated Fallacy?

For those who have reservations or criticisms regarding concerted unilateralism, four key arguments are in place:

(1) *Ambiguous Bogor Goals render "concerted unilateralism" impossible to operate*: What will APEC achieve exactly for "free and open trade and investment" by 2010 for developed economies and by 2020 for developing economies, as outlined in the Bogor Goals? Some members have taken this literally as a removal of all tariff and non-tariff barriers, and of all obstacles to foreign direct investment. Others refer to the difficulty of not being able to operationalize the goals without a clear definition, much less to benchmark specific actions for implementation. However, APEC has so far chosen not to deal with the goal definition at all.

The "constructive ambiguity" of the Bogor Goals is addressed by Andrew Elek: "the ultimate nature of free and open trade and investment, or how it was to be achieved, were not fully defined either in the Bogor Declaration or the OAA".[5] On the one hand, there has been a lack of enthusiasm from the camp of developing economies since the Asian financial crisis of 1997–98, and a new love for "ASEAN + X" scheme in the place of old familiar APEC. On the other hand, there is the no-free-lunch contention from the camp of developed economies and the new initiative for FTAAP (Free Trade Area for Asia-Pacific) in place of Bogor Goals for 2010.

(2) *Lack of specificity and contradictions in the Osaka Action Agenda (OAA); principles render no concrete measurements for evaluating compliance:*
The OAA's nine principles include: comprehensiveness; WTO-consistency; comparability; non-discrimination; transparency; standstill; simultaneous start; continuous process and differentiated timetables; flexibility; and cooperation.[6] It is not clear whether the "WTO-consistent" principle is qualified on a non-discriminatory basis or whether an exception from MFN requirements under Article XXIV would be used as a qualification. In addition, the "comprehensiveness" and "flexibility" principles could run counter to each other in that the latter undermines the commitment to exclude specific sectors from the liberalization process. Furthermore, the "concerted" element of the "concerted unilateralism" was underlined in the principle of "simultaneous start" and "continuous process" and "comparability". However, the "concerted" component is compromised by the "unilateralism" element of "differentiated timetable" and the principle of "flexibility".[7]

(3) *Failure of EVSL (Early Voluntary Sectoral Liberalization):*
The EVSL initiative is a marked case for critics to be overly cynical over the nature of "concerted unilateralism". APEC member economies could not agree on the meaning of EVSL in terms of: (a) the date by which EVSL would be finalized; (b) what was meant by "voluntary": for some governments, "voluntary" connotes the willingness to take a decision to move forward rapidly on the specified sector; for others, "voluntary" refers to an enabling clause to choose when and which sectors to commence, and at what pace, etc.; (c) the exact product coverage, and tariff codes; and most importantly, (d) the tariff levels to be reached at the end of EVSL (zero or some level between zero and 5 per cent).[8]

From my humble observation as Director (Research) at the APEC Secretariat at the time, the EVSL initiative was destined to falter due to an overdose of optimism immediately after the triumphant ITA was forwarded to the WTO in 1996, and a strong desire to launch quickly yet another APEC-to-WTO initiative.

A growing dismay intensified over the management process in the selection of 15 out of 60 plus sectors for early liberalization, and the sequential narrowing-down to target 9 sectors as priority for immediate liberalization. This unhappy situation perhaps accounted for two Latin American economies' earlier engagements in sector-nomination but eventual declining to participate in the EVSL. The conscious design of "concerted unilateralism" no doubt requires skilful leadership with a constructivist orientation of sort.

(4) *Excellent Excuse for inaction and no-progress:*
As strategic trade theorists have it, not all governments are inclined to champion for free trade, all the more so when the successful governments' protectionist measures have scored points for domestic firms. Therefore, if the rules of the game, such as "concerted unilateralism", are not concise enough, according to the critics, members would only exercise tactful compliance with the lowest common denominator. This is especially so when politicians are re-election conscious, and are unlikely to promote liberalization at the risk of alienating domestic interest groups. Furthermore, concerted liberalization would generate more domestic support if export-oriented interests are confident of gaining improved access to foreign markets. Nevertheless, unilateral liberalization would often be perceived as a loss of bargaining power in international negotiations.[9]

In sum, "concerted unilateralism", according to the critics, provides a perfect excuse for inaction and lack of progress whenever useful. The temptation to "cheat" their trading partners is therefore like the Prisoner's Dilemma game.[10] However, APEC cheerleaders and confidence-builders, including Andrew Elek, Peter Drysdale and Ross Garnaut, have faithfully argued that the unique circumstances of trade in the Asia-Pacific region have converted the traditional Prisoner's Dilemmas structure of trade cooperation into one of "Prisoner's Delight" in that the benefits of open borders to trade outweigh that of protectionism.[11] Obviously, this depends on the various inclinations of participants, as elaborated earlier.

3. Feasible Approaches to Concerted Unilateralism: A Constructivist's Perspective on the Way Forward[12]

(1) *Linking CAPs and IAPs through deductive and inductive logic:*
The inter-linkage between CAPs and IAPs is crucial for an effective working of "concerted unilateralism". There are at least two ways to establishing the linkage, one deductive and the other inductive in nature. By deductive devices, we can build in timeline benchmarks for specific agendas of CAPs. There could be flexibility, which in turn would serve as a guideline for charting and reviewing IAPs. Furthermore, by using a inductive device, APEC could gather from IAPs a substantial "critical mass" for formulating further CAPs. With deductive and inductive devices, CAPs and IAPs could supplement each other in a constructive and outcome-oriented fashion.

(2) *Integrating capacity building into the IAP review process:*
In the IAP review process, the focus could be on what current

circumstances, whether objective or perceived — constrain full implementation. The constraints could be from natural disasters, legislative restrictions, political opposition, social instability, or lack of capacity and confidence, etc. Governments could provide their respective management experience in relevant Working Groups in the context of reviewing IAPs under a specific CAP issue agenda. The APEC Travel Card scheme, for instance, has been a remarkable success. More and more member economies have steadily signed on after experiencing the sharing and capacity building. All APEC fora could build TILF and Ecotech agenda into the CAPs and respective IAPs, for developed and developing economies alike. The contents and measurements need to be managed in the spirit of "concerted unilateralism".

4. Competitive Liberalization: ITA, EVSL, and Now FTAAP

(1) *Racing into further liberation or greater confusion?*

The strategy of "competitive liberalization", chiefly crafted by C. Fred Bergsten[13] of the U.S., sustains the interaction between preferential and universal treatments on a supportive course.[14] In practice, the interchange of unilateral, bilateral, sub-regional, regional, and global trade strategies manifests itself in maximizing mutually supportive utilities. In this context, APEC is perceived as a means, not an end in itself, to achieving greater liberalization. With the anxiety over an envisaged "EU fortress" in the early 90s, there has been growing proliferation of Free Trade Agreements (FTAs).

Soon after the conclusions of the Canada-US FTA, and NAFTA, a number of US trading partners sought to negotiate comparable pacts with the US or to accede to NAFTA.[15] Furthermore, after NAFTA was concluded in 1992, President Clinton as Host of APEC in 1993, elevated APEC by initiating the annual APEC Informal Leaders Meeting, which also effectively contributed to the successful conclusion of the Uruguay Round of the WTO immediately after the APEC summit. The successful home-run of NAFTA-APEC-WTO within the 20-month duration has whetted the appetite for the pursuit of "competitive liberalization" regionally and globally. President George W. Bush's chief trade negotiator in the USTR, Robert Zoellick, articulated the trade policy as: "each of these stepping stones will ultimately lead to a trading system that creates sustainable prosperity for America, our main trading partners, and the world's developing nations".

As stated earlier, the ITA success was a boost to APEC in terms of serving as a catalyst for the WTO agenda. The EVSL was yet another attempt to stage both as a catalyst to push the stalled WTO negotiations forward and as a fall-back approach if these negotiations fail to gain further momentum. However, since the failed EVSL initiative in 1997, there has continued to be expressions of dissatisfaction. Advocates urge that APEC be geared towards a binding-APEC as opposed to sustaining a voluntary-APEC. Such proposals, including the one for APEC reform, reflect discontent over APEC's loosely organized "concerted unilateralism". In the midst of the Asian financial crisis, the lack-lustre performance of APEC led to a romanticizing of "ASEAN+3". It was evident that APEC as an institution was very much in doubt in the immediate post-EVSL period, although the flame was kept alive with an annual new host each year to put on its very best. The FTAAP (Free Trade Area of Asia Pacific) proposal was put forth in 2004 by the APEC Business Advisory Council because of the confusing rules in the regional FTAs, especially the Rules of Origins which increase business transaction costs. However, the FTAAP proposal initially received only marginal consensus, and served as a test case before it was sounded out at the Senior Officials Meeting.

(2) *FTAAP: Pros and cons of the new toy*
The proponents of an envisaged FTAAP maintained the positive aspects of their arguments:

(a) It could serve as a bargaining chip in the dismantled Doha Round of the WTO;
(b) It could serve as a fall-back approach to an aborted Round, should the Doha Round become futile in the worst-case scenario;
(c) It could integrate all the existing or emerging sub-regional FTAs/PTAs across the Asia-Pacific region, including NAFTA, FTAA, AFTA, "ASEAN+3", etc.;
(d) It could achieve the Bogor Goals of free trade and investment, given the unlikely outcome of developed economies willing to achieve them by 2010. The developed economies, according to their assessments, are not prepared to give way voluntarily without negotiations.
(e) It could somehow derail the growing interest in "ASEAN+3" by the concerned parties.

The opponents' views against the envisaged FTAAP include:

(a) It could backfire since the Doha Round of negotiations is under way. The timing couldn't be worst since APEC's sincerity in achieving a successful Round would be in question. Even if there are some merits in the envisaged FTAAP, a feasibility study should be conducted only in the case of an aborted Round.
(b) The nature of the FTAAP opposes the APEC principles, and should not be discussed under the umbrella of APEC.
(c) The FTAAP serves as an Escape Clause for the developed economies to divert from the liberalization agenda for 2010 as expected of them.
(d) The proponents are not really ready for the challenges contained in an envisaged FTAAP, therefore they are not serious.

As a face-saving device in the light of a lack of consensus, APEC members have agreed to set FTAAP as a long-term goal, and to consider possible ways to formulating it. In effect, it is a failed coup of sorts in terms of an APEC-bridged WTO bargaining chip.

(3) *FTAAP with sub-regional building blocks: A way forward?*

Given the proliferation of FTAs/RTAs within APEC region, we should insist that they serve as "building blocks" rather than "stumbling blocks" to globalization. All should be encouraged to, and not be excluded from, undertaking their desired FTAs/RTAs with implementation of CAPs/IAPs in parallel. They should harmonize their FTAs in accordance with APEC Principles on FTAs within the Bogor timeframes of 2010 and 2020. As long as there are like-minded willing partners expressing an interest, APEC should not exclude their participation. The Trans-Pacific Partnership (TPP), also known as P4 (with Brunei, Chile, New Zealand, and Singapore as initial parties), is a case in point. Competitive liberalization should be practised with a steady pace of encouragement, but not with fierce, unhealthy competition at the expense of others.

APEC as an Institution in Geopolitical Dynamics

Some critics ridiculed APEC as "A Perfect Excuse for Chats". If chats and dialogues could eventually contribute to more leadership brainstorming, more peace, and harmony; more poverty alleviation, more trade liberalization, more prosperity, and more community-building, one would certainly ask "Why not?"

As for other human constructs, APEC is not a perfect institution by itself. APEC is susceptible to various levels of discontent. APEC requires caretaking and nurturing by all participants alike. In the past two decades, APEC can boast its efforts in managing huge tasks of making the institutional architecture, formulating goals, setting agenda, coordinating opposing views, charting road maps, exerting peer pressure, and coaxing along the path of liberalization, facilitation, and economic and technical cooperation.

As the peoples of the 21 member economies are different, given variations in their individual orientation, cultural diversity, social fabric, national interests, and regional vision, it is not easy to orchestrate a coherent and harmonious APEC symphony. However, we have witnessed the participants' joint efforts in endeavours, such as the APEC Study Centres, the APEC Business Advisory Council, the APEC Secretariat, the APEC fora, and the meetings of Senior Officials, Ministers of many government agencies, and the APEC leaders. These joint efforts over the past two decades have inevitably generated successful stories where people have benefitted from the countless TILF and Ecotech agenda, such as lowering barriers to trade and investment, increasing economic growth, facilitating ease of travelling with the APEC Business Travel Card, enhancing the knowledge-based economy with APEC Digital Opportunity Centres, etc. The enormous opportunities for people-to-people contact have encouraged a strong sense of community that understands better the constraints and predicaments of other people in the region.

In the geopolitical context, APEC over the past two decades has brought enormous benefits in promoting regional peace and prosperity. The continuous engagement of the United States; the balanced inclusiveness of developed and developing members and the co-existence of China; Hong Kong, China; Chinese Taipei; the coping with a rising China; the geo-political issue agenda, such as the counter-terrorists STAR (Secure Trade in APEC Region); support during the Timor Leste's Independence; the contingency coordination during the SARS epidemics, avian influenza, and the tsunami; and the cross-strait project collaboration between China and Chinese Taipei on Emergency Preparedness and Paperless Trade, and countless others are all evidence of APEC's successes.

For whatever APEC is worth, APEC should not divert its attention from keeping its eye on the prize: participants, modality, and confidence-building. These are components of mind, body, and soul, which any institution worthy of its name should continue to nurture. The conventional geopolitical perspectives may not be the only solutions to problem solving. Whatever undertaking we devote ourselves to, be it the structure, functional architecture, or community-building, let's not forget those paths our predecessors have trodden, and the lessons learned. We should continue to work out balanced rationales and innovative solutions with a human face and constructivist approach. Last but not least, in commemoration of APEC's 20th anniversary, may all our endeavours and constructs endure the tests of challenges ahead.

Notes

1. For those who are interested in the four major theories on global governance and international cooperation — namely, liberalism, realism, constructivism, and Marxism, see Margarent P. Karns and Karen A. Mingst, *International Organizations: The Politics and Processes of Global Governance* (Lynne Rienner Publishers, Inc., 2004), pp. 35–60.
2. Barbara Koremenos, Charles Lipson, and Duncan Snidal, "The Rational Design of International Institutions", *International Organization* 55, no. 4 (Autumn, 2001): 761–99.
3. Christian Reus-Smit, *The Moral Purpose of the State: Culture, Social Identity, and Institutional Rationality in International Relations* (Princeton: Princeton University Press, 1999).
4. For a detailed discussion, see Hadi Soesastro, "APEC's Overall Goals and Objectives, Evolution and Current Status", APEC Study Center Consortium Conference (Merida, Mexico, May 2002); and Mignonne Man-jung Chan, "APEC's Concerted Unilateralism: Faith or Fallacy?" Paper presented at the APEC Study Center Consortium Conference, (Phuket, Thailand, 25–27 May 2003).

5. By 2005, this was the most well documented article with 7 annexes and comprehensive analysis on the "Mid-term Review of the Bogor Goals — Strategic Issues and Options", in *The Future of APEC and Regionalism in Asia Pacific* (CSIS/PECC, 2005). See Annex 1: The Bogor Goals, pp. 34–38.
6. "The Osaka Action Agenda: Implementation of the Bogor Declaration" (Singapore: APEC Secretariat, 1995).
7. For a more elaborate discussion, see the valuable source of reference from John Ravenhill, *APEC and the Construction of Pacific Rim Regionalism* (UK: Cambridge University Press, 2001), pp. 158–59.
8. Ibid., Ravenhill, p. 181.
9. Ibid., Ravenhill, pp. 134–38.
10. As Arthur Stein, Robert M. Axelrod, Kenneth W. Abbot, and Stephen D. Krasner would maintain.
11. Ravenhill, p. 142.
12. For detailed analysis, see Mignonne Man-jung Chan, "APEC's Concerted Unilateralism: Faith or Fallacy?" Paper presented at the APEC Study Center Consortium Conference, Thailand, 25–27 November 2003.
13. For a very useful account of competitive liberalization, see C. Fred Bergsten, "Competitive Liberalization and Global Free Trade: A Vision for the Early 21st Century", Working Paper 96-15 (Institute for International Economics, 1996); and C. Fred Bergsten, "A Renaissance for US Trade Policy", *Foreign Affairs*, November/December 2002.
14. For details, see Mignonne Man-jung Chan, "U.S. Trade Strategy of 'Competitive Liberalization' ", *Tamkang Journal of International Affairs* VIII, no. III (Jan. 2005).
15. Jeffrey J. Schott, "Understanding US Trade Policy: Circa 2001". Paper prepared at the International Affairs Institute, Rome, Italy, 18 October 2001.

References

Barbara Koremenos, Charles Lipson, and Duncan Snidal. "The Rational Design of International Institutions". International Organization 55, no. 4 (Autumn, 2001): 761–99.

C. Fred Bergsten. "A Renaissance for US Trade Policy". *Foreign Affairs*, November/December 2002.

———. "Competitive Liberalization and Global Free Trade: A Vision for the Early 21st Century". Working Paper 96-15, Institute for International Economics, 1996.

Christian Reus-Smit. *The Moral Purpose of the State: Culture, Social Identity, and Institutional Rationality in International Relations* (Princeton: Princeton University Press, 1999).

Hadi Soesastro. "APEC's Overall Goals and Objectives, Evolution and Current Status". APEC Study Center Consortium Conference (Merida, Mexico, May 2002).

John Ravenhill. *APEC and the Construction of Pacific Rim Regionalism* (UK: Cambridge University Press, 2001).

Jeffrey J. Schott. "Understanding US Trade Policy: Circa 2001". Paper Prepared at the International Affairs Institute, Rome, Italy, 18 October 2001.

Mignonne Man-jung Chan. "APEC's Concerted Unilateralism: Faith or Fallacy?" Paper presented at the APEC Study Center Consortium Conference, (Phuket, Thailand, 25–27 May 2003).

———. "U.S. Trade Strategy of 'Competitive

Liberalization' ". *Tamkang Journal of International Affairs* VIII, no. III (Jan. 2005).

Margarent P. Karns and Karen A. Mingst. *International Organizations: The Politics and Processes of Global Governance* (US: Lynne Rienner Publishers, Inc., 2004).

"Mid-term Review of the Bogor Goals — Strategic Issues and Options". In *The Future of APEC and Regionalism in Asia Pacific: Perspectives from the Second Track*, ed. Hadi Soesastro and Eduaro Pedrosa. Centre for Strategic and International Studies (CSIS) and Pacific Economic Cooperation Council (PECC).

"The Osaka Action Agenda: Implementation of the Bogor Declaration" (Singapore: APEC Secretariat, 1995).

22. Delegates are often treated to glimpses of local culture. This picture was taken during the APEC Conference on Secure Trade in the APEC Region, held in February 2003, in Bangkok, Thailand. *Photo courtesy of the APEC Secretariat.*

23. The APEC Customs-Business Dialogue held in Bangkok, Thailand, in August 2003 discussed the promotion of transparency and business confidence to implement more stringent supply chain security measures around the APEC region. *Photo Courtesy of the APEC Secretariat.*

24. APEC Economic Leaders' Meeting, Subic, Republic of the Philippines, November 1996. APEC Leaders outlined trade and investment liberalization measures to reach the Bogor Goals in the Manila Action Plans for APEC (MAPA). *Photo courtesy of the APEC Secretariat.*

25. The APEC Business Travel Card enables fast and efficient travel for business people within the APEC region and contributes to APEC's goal of free and open trade and investment. Since the scheme was created in 1997, its use has continued to accelerate steadily. By March 2008, the active number of cards was more than 34,000, with the highest share reported by Australia (nearly 40 per cent of the total number of cards issued). *Photo courtesy of the APEC Secretariat.*

5

APEC: Taking Stock and Looking Ahead

Zhang Yunling
Shen Minghui

Progress of APEC

The Asia-Pacific Economic Cooperation (APEC) forum was established in 1989 to capitalize on the growing interdependence of Asia-Pacific economies. By promoting market liberalization, facilitation and economic and technical cooperation, it intends to create a sound environment for long-term sustainable economic development and shared prosperity for all members. Its 21 member economies are home to more than 2.7 billion people and represent approximately 54 per cent of world GDP and 44 per cent of world trade. APEC has grown to become one of the world's most important regional groupings.[1]

The APEC region has gained significant progress in facilitating the trade and investment liberalization process and intra-regional trade in general. When APEC was established in 1989, the average tariff rate in the region stood at 16.9 per cent. By 2004 barriers had been reduced by approximately 70 per cent to 5.5 per cent.[2] Since APEC's inception, APEC's total trade has grown almost 4 times, GDP tripled, significantly outpacing the rest of the world.[3] With the more liberalized market environment, the intra-APEC trade (exports and imports) has grown rapidly, from US$1.7 trillion in 1989 to US$8.44 trillion in 2007 — an average increase of 8.5 per cent per year, accounting for 67 per cent in 2007.

The composition of APEC's membership is a novel arrangement as it has brought together developing, newly industrializing and advanced industrial economies into a process of regional consultation and cooperation.[4] To 21

APEC member economies, APEC is a unique forum, operating on the basis of open dialogue and respect for the views of all participants. It is a unique regional institution committed to reducing barriers to trade and investment following the approach of voluntary actions and enhancing the economic and technical cooperation aiming at capacity building and reducing the economic development gaps, i.e. by individual action plans (IAPs) without requiring its members to enter into legally binding obligations and collective action plans (CAPs) based on the members' commitments.

Although APEC is a regional forum without powers of management, it has established well functioning mechanisms for consultation and cooperation. At a policy level, APEC is directed by the 21 APEC Economic Leaders. Strategic recommendations are provided by APEC Ministers, as well as the APEC Business Advisory Council (ABAC).[5] At a working level, APEC's activities and projects are guided by APEC Senior Official Meetings (SOM). Several high level committees have been established at the working level, for example, the Committee on Trade and Investment (CTI), and the Budget and Management Committee (BMC). In addition, Sub-Committees, Experts' Groups, Working Groups and Task Forces all support the activities and projects led by these high-level committees. The APEC Policy Support Unit provides research, analysis and evaluation capabilities to assist in the implementation of APEC's agenda. The APEC process is supported by a permanent Secretariat based in Singapore though it is still limited in size and functional activities.[6]

APEC's activities are focused on three key areas: trade and investment liberalization, business facilitation, and economic and technical cooperation. The programmes that APEC has designed and conducted enable APEC member economies to share ideas and improve their policy making.[7]

In order to achieve progress in the above three activities, a series of important initiatives have been endorsed by APEC member economies within a period of two decades. One of the important functions of APEC is to create initiatives to realize the above three goals. The following are the major initiatives:

— The Bogor Goals of "free and open trade and investment in the Asia-Pacific by 2010 for industrialized economies and 2020 for developing economies" (Bogor, Indonesia in 1994).
— The Osaka Action Agenda (OAA) providing a framework for meeting the Bogor Goals through trade and investment liberalization, business facilitation and sectoral activities, underpinned by policy dialogues and economic and technical cooperation (Osaka, Japan in 1995).
— The Manila Action Plan for APEC (MAPA) outlining the trade and investment liberalization and facilitation measures to reach the Bogor Goals. In addition, the first Collective and Individual Action

Plans are compiled, outlining how economies will achieve the free trade goals (Manila, Philippines, in 1996).

- The proposal for early voluntary sectoral liberalization (EVSL) in 15 sectors and the decision of updating Individual Action Plans annually (Vancouver, Canada, in 1997).
- The first nine sectors for EVSL (Kuala Lumpur, Malaysia, in 1998).
- APEC commitments of paperless trading by 2005 in developed economies and 2010 in developing economies; APEC Business Travel Card scheme; Mutual Recognition Arrangement on Electrical Equipment; and a Framework for the Integration of Women in APEC (Auckland, New Zealand, in 1999).
- Establishment of electronic Individual Action Plan (e-IAP) system (Bandar Seri Begawan, Brunei Darussalam, in 2000).
- The Shanghai Accord focusing on Broadening the APEC Vision, Clarifying the Roadmap to Bogor and Strengthening the Implementation Mechanism in addition to the e-APEC Strategy and APEC's first Counter-Terrorism Statement (Shanghai, People's Republic of China in 2001).
- Trade Facilitation Action Plan I, APEC's second Counter-Terrorism Statement and the Secure Trade in the APEC Region (STAR) Initiative (Los Cabos, Mexico in 2002).
- The APEC Action Plan on SARS and the Health Security Initiative (Bangkok, Thailand in 2003).
- The Best Practices for RTAs and FTAs and the Santiago Initiative for Expanded Trade and a Data Privacy Framework (Santiago, Chile in 2004).
- The Busan Roadmap, the Mid-Term Stocktake finding that APEC is well on its way to meeting the Bogor Goals, and the APEC Privacy Framework (Busan, Korea in 2005).
- The Ha Noi Action Plan identifying specific actions and milestones to implement the Bogor Goals and support capacity building measures to help APEC economies (Ha Noi, Vietnam in 2006).
- Declaration on Climate Change, Energy Security and Clean Development, the report on closer Regional Economic Integration including structural reform initiatives, and Trade Facilitation Action Plan II reducing trade transaction costs by a further 5 per cent by 2010 (Sydney, Australia in 2007).
- The APEC Investment Facilitation Action Plan aimed at improving the investment environment in the region (Lima, Peru in 2008).

Moreover, APEC as a regional institution plays an active role in dealing with emerging crises and challenges, for example, in the 1997 Asian financial crisis, the current global financial/economic crisis, and also the environment and climate change issues. During the Asian financial crisis in 1997, APEC Finance Ministers discussed measures to be implemented to contain the crisis and encouraged the provision of financial and technical assistance bilaterally to the affected economies. APEC also attached importance to capital market development, capital account liberalization, and strengthening international financial systems. It supported efforts to improve surveillance of financial sector supervisory regimes and welcomed better coordination or cooperation ways, like peer review, to strengthen the existing global mechanisms. In addition, the Basel Core Principles on Effective Banking Supervision, the report on Financial Stability in Emerging Market Economies prepared by the G-10 in collaboration with a number of emerging market economies were endorsed by the Ministers.

Some measures were also endorsed by Ministers in the areas of financial systems. For instance, two action plans for strengthening the training of bank supervisors and securities regulators in APEC economies were endorsed. In addition, some training initiatives like the joint initiative of Canada and the World Bank to establish the Toronto International Leadership Centre for Financial Sector Supervision, the opening of the ADB Institute in Tokyo, the IMF-Singapore Regional Training Institute (STI), and bilateral training assistance provided by individual economies as well as the initiative of the APEC Financiers Group to create a private-sector training and education program for financiers across the APEC region were all encouraged and supported by APEC.[8]

However, APEC has experienced a difficult transition in light of new developments in the Asia-Pacific region. APEC had an ambitious goal to turn the Asia-Pacific into a region of free trade and investment by 2010 for the developed members and by 2020 for the developing members. The 1997 Asian financial crisis, however, forced its members to shift their priorities to stabilize and reform the financial sector and stimulate economic growth. After the 1997 financial crisis, with the emerging trend of FTAs, APEC members then diverted their efforts to negotiate bilateral FTA/EPAs. Although APEC members have shown their full support for the DDA, its role seems limited to pushing the process to an early success. Again, the current global financial/economic crisis has made APEC members focus on effective measures to fix their financial sector and to stimulate economic growth. The G-20, which is made up of major economies on the global level, has come to play an important role in promoting reforms in the international financial system and to restructure the path of economic growth. To some extent, the APEC process has lost its momentum in realizing its designed goal and in playing a key role in the regional integration and cooperation process.

Challenges to APEC

A significant challenge to APEC is how to realize the Bogor Goals. Based on the "open regionalism" principle, the implementation of liberalization and facilitation in the APEC region is conducted through unilateral actions (IAPs). But the "concerted unilateral liberalization" (CUL) has shown weakness in implementation as member economies do not feel obliged until their neighbours have achieved progress in the areas towards the Bogor Goals. This soft approach makes the Bogor Goals unrealizable though there has been peer pressure for review under APEC agenda.

The Asian financial crisis in 1997 and the stalled Doha Development Agenda (DDA) negotiation, also had a negative effect on the progress towards realizing the Bogor Goals. The Asian financial crisis in 1997 hit the economies and dragged down the growth of the APEC member economies significantly. Faced with an economic downturn, as well as shrinking outer markets, the priority of APEC members shifted to economic recovery and reform of its financial sector. As a result, the effort to promote market liberalization through joint actions through the Early Voluntary Sector Liberalization (EVSL) initiative in nine sectors failed. After the Asian financial crisis, the momentum of pushing market liberalization aiming at achieving the Bogor Goals seemed lost because of lack of strong support from APEC members. APEC members were unwilling to go further in the pursuit of liberalization, because of their limited commitment to APEC (which was subject to WTO commitments). Expectations are that the DDA must be resolved; otherwise; it is difficult for APEC members' unilateral actions plans to make breakthroughs in liberalization. This may have ultimately affected the realization of the Bogor Goals.[9] According to the Bogor agenda, APEC developed member economies should realize their commitments by 2010. Nevertheless, no actions seem to have been taken by any developed member economy.

The challenge is that either the Bogor Goals will have to be restructured if APEC wants to continue its effort to promote the region's trade and investment liberalization process, or the goals and functions of APEC have to be reoriented. At the same time, it is important to keep the spirit and long-term goal for a free trade and investment region and create new initiatives towards an FTAAP by the time all members agree to do so.

Another challenge for APEC has been to realize its commitment of reducing economic development gaps among all its member economies. The aim of APEC's activities through its trade/investment liberalization process, facilitation and economic and technical cooperation was to narrow gaps in economic development, by helping to enhance the capacities of its less developed members. However, development gaps among APEC members have increased. For example, GDP per capita in most economies have doubled, and some like China have increased by up to 10 times, while member economies like Papua New Guinea have stayed almost the same from 1989 to 2008. Growth has been uneven among developing member economies, and not all have benefited equally from the APEC process. If this trend continues, it is argued that APEC may lead into a dead-end, without interest and support from the developing member economies.[10]

For instance, GDP per capita of Australia in 1989 was $17,955, and it increased to $47,400 in 2008. Australia became the richest economy in terms of its per capita in the APEC region. In contrast, the GDP per capita of Vietnam in 1998 was $361, and increased to $1,040 in 2008. Vietnam, however, remains the least developed economy among APEC members. In 1989, the GDP per capita of Japan, the richest economy in the region, was almost 33.7 times that of the Philippines, the poorest in the region; while in 2008, the gap widened to 45.6 times between the richest, Australia and the poorest, Vietnam.

Unlike traditional Official Development Assistance (ODA), APEC provides the assistance to less developed members through the economic and technical cooperation (ECOTEC) process. Capacity building through participation, training and best practices are considered the most effective ways for enhancing the level of skills and abilities present in developing economies. Nevertheless, the role of seminars, discussions and even some training by APEC seem to be not very effective in strengthening their capacities, since the dominant players in the economy are multinational corporations (MNCs). As such, APEC should strengthen its role in social programmes.

A new challenge to APEC is how to reduce the negative effect of the "noodle bowl" (spaghetti bowl effect) caused by the multilayered bilateral and sub-regional FTAs/EPAs. The economies of APEC members are highly interdependent, either through a regional production network in East Asia, or through trade networks between East Asia and the North America. The production network operates by separating a production chain into small parts and then assigning each to the most cost-efficient location. This means that production processes will be fragmented into multiple parts and located in different countries in East Asia. Some production steps take place within a single firm (or firms of the same group) that has operations in different countries, while others involve arm's length transactions among different firms in several countries. FTAs on the other hand are arranged in the Asia-Pacific region with a multi-layered approach. This approach gives individual partner incentives to bargain for its special concerns and interests during the negotiations and implementation. The sub-regional group, like ASEAN has concluded several "ASEAN+I" FTAs , aiming at ensuring its super position and advantage, as well as realizing its best-expected gain. However, the web of bilateral FTAs has created new barriers to regional trade and investment. The regional market has become divided because of different arrangements, which will reduce the gains from the scale of the regional market. Business costs will increase due to the complicated or contradictory regulations (for example, rules of origin or ROOs), which are counter-productive to the network-based economic integration.

Complex FTAs in the APEC region could potentially disrupt the processes of cross-border production networks which have been central to the region's successful integration and do harm to the smooth trading environment. Uncoordinated proliferation may lead to inconsistent provisions between FTAs, especially on the rules of origin, which could hamper the process of production networks across countries.[11]

The transaction costs related to border-crossing procedures in an FTA may increase. Such costs are related to documenting products and verifying them prior to crossing the border. Continuous treatment of transactions across borders could be cumbersome, and hence may not be effective to promote exchange in an FTA. Necessary documents to prove the origin of exchange entails costs which may cause producers to pay relevant duties rather than incur the costs of proving origin.

The "noodle bowl" effects of FTAs has happened for two reasons: one is that the scope and models of tariff liberalization arrangements vary in each agreement, while another is differences in the ROOs. FTAs have different phase-in modalities, i.e., tariff reduction schedule. Thus an exporter faces different tariffs depending on the destination. As for the ROOs, there are several types, and they are used differently even in a same agreement. The complex arrangement of ROOs in the APEC region adds red tape and costs to firms in the APEC region.

There are also concerns that the proliferation of bilateral and sub-regional FTAs in the Asia-Pacific region may run counter to the regional goals of trade and investment liberalization. APEC could try to play a role in mitigating the noodle bowl effect by standardizing FTAs. But this may not work well since enforcement may not be possible and each negotiation is different in structure and time schedule. One option is to encourage APEC to initiate some facilitation projects by integrating or even harmonizing some rules, for example, an APEC-wide rule of origin (ROO) arrangement, or a consolidated ROO standard (for example, the so-called co-equal rule).

China's Participation and Role

The Asia-Pacific region is the most important region for China's economic external engagement, and it is the major market for China's external trade and source of FDI inflows. As the first regional institution in which China has participated, APEC plays a special role for China to learn and to exercise its unilateral liberalization efforts.

The APEC region also provides more than 60 per cent of China's export and import market, as well as FDI inflow market. Of the top 10 largest trading partners, 8 of them are from the APEC region; 6 of the top 10 largest investors were members of APEC as of 2008. Before becoming a member of the WTO, China's unilateral liberalization programmes were all announced at the APEC forum. As a regional forum organizing many kinds of programmes, discussions and initiatives, China has gained experience from its participation, and has also been gradually making initiatives either in the areas of capacity building or economic and technical assistance. For example, China benefited from APEC in the reform of its domestic laws and regulations, integration with international trade practices, and the standardization of market competition, etc. Discussions and commitments relating to business performance, intellectual property rights, government procurement, capacity building etc. in the APEC fora have helped Chinese officials and experts expand their knowledge and improve their skills.

With the enriched experiences and successful development of its economy, China has become more and more confident and active in participating in the APEC process. One example is China's successful leadership in organizing the 9th Leaders' Meeting and related programmes which were held successfully in Shanghai in 2001: the outcome was the Shanghai Accord and several other important documents. APEC members agreed on the new agenda for broadening the APEC vision, clarifying the roadmap to Bogor and strengthening the implementation mechanism as well as the e-APEC Strategy. In addition, APEC's first Counter-Terrorism Statement was issued that strengthened the political role of APEC.[12] In facing the current financial/economic crisis, China took the leading role and also called on cooperative actions to stabilize the financial sector, to stimulate the domestic demand and to oppose protectionism.[13]

China will continue to have a strong interest to participate in APEC activities and to support it by playing a positive role in promoting regional economic integration and cooperation.

Concluding Remarks

Considering the great diversity of APEC members, it is not realistic to expect that APEC can initiate an APEC wide FTA agenda based on negotiations in the near future. In 2006, then President Bush of the United States called for an agenda of the Free Trade Area of the Asia-Pacific (FTAAP). It received little support from APEC members. It seems that a real free trade and investment environment in the Asia-Pacific region will be a long-term goal. However, this does not mean that APEC should give up its goal to create a dynamic economic region based on free trade and investment.

In facing the new challenges, APEC should revise its priorities by endorsing more programmes on facilitation, capacity building and collective action-oriented projects on new issues like energy and climate change.

APEC should become more active and effective in dealing with the current financial crisis, reform of the international financial system, domestic reforms on both financial and economic structures, as well as the post-crisis agendas, like a sustainable and balanced trade structure and relations in the Asia-Pacific region.

APEC's future will continue with support from all members if it re-designs its position and role in the new global context.

Notes

1. APEC. *APEC at a Glance 2009*, p. 2.
2. APEC. *A Mid-Term Stocktake of the Bogor Goals*, 2005.
3. Department of Foreign Affairs & Trade, Australia. *The APEC Region Trade and Investment 2008.*
4. Antonina Ivanova and Manuel Angeles. Trade and environment issues in APEC, *The Social Science Journal* 43 (2006): 629–42.
5. ABAC, formed by the business leaders, is considered an important part of the APEC process.
6. APEC. *APEC at a Glance 2009*, p. 4.
7. Ibid., p. 5.
8. See APEC Finance Ministers, Joint Ministerial Statement, Kananaskis, Canada, May 1998.
9. Lu Jianren. "The Five Big Challenges to APEC in Coming Years". *World Economy Review*, no. 4 (2004).
10. Zhang Yunling et al. *Focus on Shanghai: the progress and perspective of APEC (in Chinese)*, pp. 5-6 (Beijing: Economy and Management Publishing House, 2001).
11. Tubagus Fereidhanusetyawan. "Preferential Trade Agreements in the Asia-Pacific Region". *IMF Working Paper 05149*, p. 31, 2005.
12. APEC. *APEC Outcomes and Outlook 2008–2009*, p. 25.
13. Hu Jintao, speech at the 16th APEC informal Leaders' Meeting, 23 Nov. 2008. <www. fmprc.gov.cn>.

26. VIP delegates visiting the APEC Secretariat Library on the day of the official opening of the APEC Secretariat on 6 September 2003. *Photo courtesy of the APEC Secretariat.*

27. Mr Bob Hawke, Australian Prime Minister, was among the regional leaders who led the Public Globalization Debate at the APEC Secretariat Building Opening in Singapore on 6 September 2003. *Photo courtesy of the APEC Secretariat.*

28. The First Senior Officials' Meeting held in Santiago, Chile, from 2 to 3 March 2004 discussed among other matters, the political support for the successful conclusion of the Doha Development Agenda, and the formulation of a proposal to address Free Trade Agreements/Regional Trade Agreements in the APEC region. *Photo courtesy of the APEC Secretariat.*

29. SOM III and Related Meetings group photograph. The meetings were held from 25 September to 4 October 2004 in Santiago, Chile, and discussed a host of issues including trade and investment issues, tourism, and biotech strategies. *Photo courtesy of the APEC Secretariat.*

30. The Second Senior Officials' Meeting and Related Meetings held in Jeju, Korea to discuss the "Mid-term Stocktaking of Progress towards the Bogor Goals" on 28 May 2005. *Photo courtesy of the APEC Secretariat.*

31. APEC Leaders' Meeting, Shanghai, China, October 2001. APEC Leaders adopted the Shanghai Accord which broadened the APEC vision to include measures to counter terrorism. *Photo courtesy of the APEC Secretariat.*

6

Revamping APEC's Concerted Unilateral Liberalization

Hadi Soesastro

Introduction

The opportunity will not come twice for countries in the diverse Asia-Pacific region to engage in a productive regional trade agenda as provided by APEC's Concerted Unilateral Liberalization (CUL). This unique approach has found its manifestation in the annual submission of Individual Action Plans (IAPs) covering 15 areas of trade and investment liberalization and facilitation. They were first introduced in 1996 as the principal mechanism to realize the Bogor Goals of "free and open trade and investment in the region" by 2010 for the developed members and 2020 for the developing members of APEC.

The 1994 APEC Bogor Goals "is to this day APEC's best known and most important decision" (Damond 2003, p. 89). It was the apex of a strong process that began with the first APEC Economic Leaders Meeting on Blake Island (Seattle) that articulated the vision of the Asia Pacific as a region of free trade and investment. The following year, when APEC leaders reconvened in Bogor (Indonesia), they committed themselves to creating "free and open trade and investment in the region" by a certain date. In arriving at this decision, the leaders were assisted by an Eminent Persons Group (EPG) that produced three consecutive reports (APEC 1993, 1994, 1995). The EPG worked closely with a group of "sherpas" that directly assisted the leaders.

It was this "leaders track" that produced the bold initiative, but the modality to implement the Bogor Goals was crafted through a process within the "normal track" in APEC. This process, managed by Ministers and Senior Officials, did interact intensively with various "second track" activities like the Pacific Economic Cooperation Council (PECC), the Pacific Basin Economic Council (PBEC), as well as a multi-country group of scholars organized by the Australia-Japan Research Centre at the Australian National University.[1] This process has led to the formulation and adoption of APEC's concerted unilateral approach in 1995 that defines the Osaka Action Agenda (OAA) and became the main modality to realize the Bogor Goals. Subsequently, at the 1996 meeting the leaders endorsed the Manila Action Plan for APEC that marked the beginning of the OAA's implementation stage with the initial submission of Individual Action Plans (IAPs) by APEC members.

The speed with which a vision was turned into action was unprecedented. That was APEC's heyday. It will not be easy to repeat this kind of development in APEC or any other regional cooperation arrangements in East Asia, but important lessons can again and again be learnt from that experience. It is also remarkable that no single APEC country has since failed to produce the yearly IAP. The IAPs are designed to produce "peer pressure" that will result in a process of progressive "unilateral liberalization", which should happens in a "concerted" manner since it is organized with a common framework.

Several independent studies to assess APEC IAPs over the years (Yamazawa 1998; PECC 1999; Yamazawa and Urata 2000; and Woo 2003) have concluded that the results have been less spectacular than expected. The value-added of the IAPs has been questioned (Bergsten 2004), but despite the growing disappointment, it was felt that APEC should not abandon this modality. Chan (2005) argued that concerted unilateralism is an imperative for a region with such diverse members as the Asia Pacific and therefore, the region cannot afford to do so. Accepting this fact, Han (2005) was of the view that the process does not provide sufficient incentives for APEC members to implement their commitments. The Bogor Goals, he argued, created a dilemma for a voluntary arrangement like APEC to implement. Ways have to be found to overcome this problem.

This chapter begins with a brief review of the issues that arose when the Bogor Goals were crafted. This will help explain the adoption of the concept of concerted unilateral liberalization and the challenges the region has encountered to putting it into practice. It then examines the process to operationalize this concept and efforts over the years to improve it. A "peer review" process was introduced in 1998 that marked the start of a "concerted" mode to reinforcing the drive towards unilateral liberalization in the region. The chapter concludes with an examination of areas for consideration in strengthening this peer review process. This is a key element to revamping APEC's concerted unilateral liberalization.

The Bogor Goals: What, Why, and How

The issuance in 1994 of the APEC Economic Leaders' Declaration of Common Resolve, or the Bogor Declaration, has been heralded as providing a major impetus for moving the APEC process forward. The Declaration contains eleven points. Of these, the one relating to the goal of free and open trade and investment in the region (the Bogor Goals) was the most contentious issue. The leaders did not provide a clear definition of what these goals meant in practice but they agreed on the following principles:

- The goal will be pursued promptly by further reducing barriers to trade and investment and by promoting the free flow of goods, services, and capital among APEC economies;
- This goal will be achieved in a GATT-consistent manner;
- This goal will be achieved no later than the year 2020;
- The pace of implementation will take into account the differing levels of economic development among APEC economies, with the industrialized economies achieving the goal no later than the year 2010 and developing countries no later than the year 2020;
- APEC opposes the creation of an inward-looking trading bloc that would divert from the pursuit of global free trade and the APEC goal will be pursued in a manner that will encourage and strengthen trade and investment liberalization in the world as a whole;
- The outcome of APEC liberalization will be not only the actual reduction of barriers among APEC economies but also that between APEC economies and non-APEC economies; and
- Particular attention will be given to trade with non-APEC developing countries to ensure that they will benefit from APEC liberalization in conformity with GATT/WTO provisions.

The Declaration also did not specify the modality by which the goal will be achieved. In the process of crafting the Declaration it became clear that there was no appetite for creating a free trade area (FTA) and that its political feasibility was almost nil. A number of options were proposed but they were not formally discussed in the meeting (of the Leaders as well as the Ministers) perhaps because it was felt that differences of views on how the goal should be achieved were too wide. The APEC EPG proposed a kind of compromise, namely *negotiated liberalization among APEC members* — a *de facto* kind of free trade area — that can be extended to non-members only on a mutually reciprocal basis.[2] *Individual members* can unilaterally extend APEC liberalization to non-members on an unconditional MFN basis.

To prevent an implicit endorsement of the EPG proposal in the Bogor

Declaration, Malaysia and Thailand issued their interpretation of the APEC (Bogor) goals.[3] In essence they want to convey that the EPG proposal was not in accordance to their understanding of what "open regionalism" was. President Kim Young Sam of Korea expressed his strong commitment to supporting free trade in the region on a non-discriminatory or MFN basis (*Straits Times*, 8 November 1994). Prime Minister Keating further stated that APEC's rationale is to prevent the creation of a discriminatory trade bloc (*The Times*, 4 November 1994).

Malaysia's submission contained the following points:

- the liberalization process to achieve the goal will not create an exclusive free trade area in the Asia-Pacific;
- the liberalization process will be GATT/WTO-consistent and on an unconditional MFN basis;
- the target dates of 2020 and 2010 are indicative dates and non-binding on member economies;
- the liberalization process to be undertaken will be on a best endeavour basis;
- APEC member economies will liberalize their trade and investment regime based on their capacity to undertake such liberalization commensurate with their level of development; and
- the liberalization process will cover only a substantial portion of Asia-Pacific trade and should not go beyond the provisions of GATT/WTO.

Thailand made the following remarks:

- the goal is not to create a free trade area, and APEC liberalization must proceed in consonance with the decision of the Uruguay Round and the WTO;
- the time frame specified should be seen as the target for achieving the goal; and
- the "elimination" of trade and investment barriers in the region should be done on a gradual basis.

It was reported that the United States also objected to the 2010 date but it finally gave in because it realized that at that stage it would be difficult for Indonesia to accommodate all the changes (*Far Eastern Economic Review*, 24 November 1994). In a press interview (*Straits Times*, 16 November 1994), Malaysia's Prime Minister Mahathir, suggested that as Chairman of the APEC meeting, President Soeharto wanted to avoid too many changes to the Declaration and therefore suggested that differing opinions should be expressed in the form of an annexure to the Declaration. Mahathir was of the view that the annexure was part of the Bogor Declaration. Prime Minister Goh Chok Tong of Singapore and Prime Minister Keating of Australia did not agree to that (*Straits Times*, 17 November 1994). It was reported that Indonesia would issue an annex to the Declaration that would address several outstanding issues, including North Asian concerns over agricultural liberalization (*Far Eastern*

Economic Review, 24 November 1994). In the end there was no annex to the Declaration. However, the concerns expressed by Malaysia and Thailand appeared to have been taken into account in subsequent development of the modality to achieve the Bogor Goals.

The nature of the agreement was another issue that created some controversy. Skeptics questioned the purpose of having an agreement that is not legally binding (*Asian Wall Street Journal*, 9 November 1994). The chairman of the APEC EPG, Fred Bergsten, argued that the Bogor Declaration should be seen primarily as a political commitment (*Asiaweek*, 23 November 1994). A senior U.S. official, Winston Lord, believed that the value of the political commitment was in its ability to create momentum to trade liberalization (*Bangkok Post*, 5 November 1994). Prime Minister Goh Chok Tong also argued that once a country made a political commitment it had to try to implement it (*Straits Times*, 17 November 1994). Prime Minister Mahathir was also concerned about the implications of this understanding of the leaders' political commitment and included in the Malaysian reservation that APEC decisions must be based on consensus.

The issue of the consensus decision-making procedure in APEC arose right from the outset of the APEC meetings in Indonesia when triggered off by U.S. objections at the SOM to the wording of APEC's non-binding investment principles (Soesastro 1997). In addressing this issue, President Soeharto proposed that decisions should be reached on the basis of a "broad consensus", meaning that a decision would as much as possible become a general consent enabling countries that are ready to implement it to do so immediately while those that are less prepared would follow later on (*Jakarta Post*, 12 November 1994). Thailand's Deputy Prime Minister, Supachai, proposed a "pragmatic consensus", while Prime Minister Goh Chok Tong suggested that APEC should work on the basis of a "flexible consensus" and that a "consensus does not necessarily mean unanimity" (*Straits Times*, 17 November 1994).

Malaysia felt that the terms "broad, pragmatic, and flexible consensus" were sought to give others the sanction to proceed with the proposal even when there were a few dissenting voices. The question is whether in APEC a proposal could proceed even without Malaysia's consent (*New Strait Times*, 14 November 1994). This issue aroused further discussion about the so-called opt-out option, and specifically on allowing Malaysia to opt out. In the end it appeared that "flexible consensus" was understood as an agreement by all to adopt an APEC plan or programme but that individual APEC members can defer their participation in the respective plan or programme.

The above review clearly underlines the conclusion of the 1996 PECC study that APEC's realistic role in trade liberalization should be the reinforcement of the process of unilateral liberalization: "APEC rides on, and mainly reinforces, the liberalization wave sweeping the Asia-Pacific region rather than being the leading force." The APEC strategy of liberalization based on a concerted unilateral approach appears to be the only feasible modality at that stage. This strategy, however, should be seen in light of APEC's evolutionary approach. The value added of the approach lies in the success of the group to encourage all members to liberalize further and faster than those already agreed under the multilateral trading system (WTO).

There was the belief that this process could bring about progressive unilateral liberalization in the region, noting that several countries in the region already moved in that direction. When introducing its 1995 budget the Malaysian Government announced a further tariff-cutting exercise of over 2,600 items. In early January 1995 Thailand also announced the further reduction of tariffs on around 3,000 items. In May 1995, and again in June 1996, Indonesia issued packages of across-the-board trade deregulation with schedules of tariff reductions to the year 2003.

Implementing Concerted Unilateral Liberalization

In their 1996 Statement, APEC Ministers noted that Individual Action Plans (IAPs) represented the member economies' individual voluntary commitments and the first concrete steps taken by them to put into action their commitment towards achieving APEC's long-term goal of free and open trade and investment. They further noted the "rolling nature" of the IAPs and the importance of continuing consultations and annual review in order to sustain the process of voluntary improvements of the IAPs. Implicitly, they counted on the effectiveness of "peer pressure".

Indeed, at the APEC SOM in Cebu in May 1996 when first drafts of the IAPs were presented, the Indonesian SOM Chair found out that Indonesia's offers were less progressive than those of several other member economies that are seen as reference. He was embarrassed about that and thought that Indonesia should immediately revise its IAP.[4] It should also be noted that the consultations were conducted in closed meetings on a bilateral basis in order not to embarrass any member economy. By the end of 1996 IAPs were submitted for their implementation starting on 1 January 1997.

The IAPs contain 15 chapters relating to the 15 issue areas specified in the Osaka Action Agenda (OAA) and are now available to the public (www.apec-iap.org). The 15 issue areas are: tariffs, non-tariff measures, services, investment, standards and conformance, customs procedures, intellectual property, competition policy, government procurement, deregulation/regulatory review, WTO obligations, rules of origin, dispute mediation, mobility of business people, and information gathering and analysis. Each chapter in the IAP contains three main sections, namely: (a) an overview that contains a summary of an economy's current policy approach in an issue area, including highlights of any significant improvements that have occurred over the past 12 months; (b) an annual report that provides details of action taken over the last 12 months to improve trade and investment liberalization and facilitation, the current policy approach/arrangements and further improvements planned; and (c) a base year and cumulative improvements table to give an accurate picture of the progress being made by an economy towards the Bogor Goals in a particular issue area.

Throughout 1997 the process of consultations on the IAPs continued to be conducted bilaterally. APEC Ministers Responsible for Trade (MRT) agreed to use IAPs to: (a) describe member economies' commitments and intentions for moving to liberalize restrictions, facilitate trade and establish business-friendly policy regimes; and (b) describe in a transparent manner future directions that can guide business and investment decisions. This agreement was taken up by the APEC Business Advisory Council (ABAC) that pointed to the need that the IAPs demonstrate value added (to commitment by the respective members elsewhere), transparency, specificity, and commitment to action. APEC Ministers responded by agreeing to improve the format of the IAPs to ensure greater transparency, facilitate review and assessment and enhance their usefulness to the business community.

In 1998 major improvements were made to the process. Although bilateral consultations continued, a process of "peer review" was introduced in conjunction with SOMs. This was an important step to increasing transparency and in turn also "peer pressure". Several countries, starting with Korea and Malaysia, submitted themselves to a voluntary peer review process. However, the result of this process was not disclosed to outsiders. It should be noted that member economies, including those affected by the financial crisis, continued to make improvements in their IAPs.[5]

The Japan member committee of PECC was the first to initiate an independent assessment of 1997 IAPs that became publicly available (Yamazawa, 1998). In 1999 APEC itself undertook an assessment of the overall progress and PECC was also asked to do a review of the IAPs. PECC showed that APEC member economies were continuing to make reasonable progress towards the attainment of APEC objectives in a number of areas with little backsliding, but there was a need for improved performance in a number of areas (PECC 1999). However, in presenting their work PECC was asked by APEC not to name member economies. In its assessment of progress, the APEC Ministerial Statement informed that 18 member economies have implemented significant tariff reductions, 12 member economies made improvements in the area of NTBs, 17 member economies further liberalized their investment regimes, and 18 member economies made improvements in the areas of competition policy and deregulation. No information was given about which member economies made progress because this would reveal the member economies that failed to perform. APEC Ministers, however, recognized the need for guidelines on how member economies could show how they intend to achieve the Bogor Goals, realizing perhaps that IAPs were mainly reporting on measures that they had taken already.

In 2000 new IAP format guidelines were approved. Also, the e-IAP initiative was launched to enable member economies to upload their annual submission to the IAP Website. This allows for easy access by the public to the IAPs, and is specially aimed at assisting the business community to plan with more certainty and to benefit more quickly from the actions planned.

Besides steps to improve the e-IAP system a major initiative was taken in 2001 to develop more rigorous monitoring and assessment by organizing so-called IAP Review Teams. The APEC Shanghai Accord of 2001 identified the need to place the Bogor Goals within the context of an undated and expanded vision that addressed both trade and investment liberalization and facilitation (TILF) and economic and technical cooperation (ECOTECH) "in an integrated manner to maximize the befits for all economies in the region". In clarifying the roadmap to Bogor, the Shanghai Accord adopted a pathfinder approach in advancing selected APEC initiatives towards achieving the Bogor Goals. It also identified concrete actions and measures to reduce transaction costs by 5 per cent across the APEC region over five years.

Since 2002 the IAP Review Team has included an independent expert who is commissioned to prepare a study report, and the private sector was invited to the SOMs to make comments on the IAPs. This was a major development in the process.

As can be seen from Table 6.1, 2002 was the beginning of the first three-year cycle of the enhanced APEC peer review process. All member economies were subjected to a peer review, and they agreed to complete the peer review of all 21 member economies by the time of SOM I in 2005 so that a Mid-Term Stocktake (MTST) towards achieving the Bogor Goals could be conducted.

An independent assessment of the enhanced peer review process was undertaken by Woo Yuen Pau in 2003. This assessment study highlighted key unresolved issues in the peer review process. The first issue addressed the need for a consistent methodology to assessing the IAPs submitted by different member economies. The second issue was on the question of the value added of this APEC process. Woo (2003) thought that the peer review process had not been sufficiently focused on the unilateral steps that members intended to take towards meeting the Bogor Goals. The third issue, which follows from the above, was whether the IAP is more like a *trade policy report* (similar to those produced by the WTO) or whether it should really be an *action plan*. Apparently in the course of the exercise the IAPs became less of an action plan than a report of measures that had been taken in the past year. The fourth issue related to a "design flaw" of the IAPs and the need to

TABLE 6.1
Developments of the IAP Peer Review Process

Origin and Pre-Launch	
1994	Bogor Goals
1995	Osaka Action Agenda: Agreeing on IAPs as the modality
1996	Manila Action Plan: Initial submission of IAPs
1997	Implementation of IAPs
Voluntary Peer Review of IAPs	
1997 — SOM II	Launch of IAP Peer Review
1998	Korea, Malaysia
1999	Australia, Brunei Darussalam
2000	China, Indonesia, Mexico, Peru, Singapore, Chinese Taipei, Thailand
2001	Canada, Russia
2002 – SOM I	Preparation to launch enhanced peer review
First Cycle of Enhanced Peer Review (with Report by Independent Expert)	
2002 – SOM III	Japan, Mexico
2003 – SOM I	Australia, Canada, Thailand
2003 – SOM III	Hong Kong (China), Korea, New Zealand
2004 – SOM I	Chile, China, Peru, United States
2004 – SOM III	Singapore, Chinese Taipei
2005 – SOM I	Brunei Darussalam, Indonesia, Malaysia, Papua New Guinea, Philippines, Russia, Viet Nam
2005	Bogor Goals' Mid-term Stock Taking
2006	Preparation to launch the second round of enhanced peer review
Second Cycle of Enhanced Peer Review (with Report by two Independent Experts)	
2007 – SOM I	Australia, Hong Kong (China), Japan, Chinese Taipei
2007 – SOM III	China, Korea, New Zealand
2008 – SOM I	Canada, United States
2008 – SOM II	Chile, Mexico, Peru, Singapore
2009 – SOM I	Brunei Darussalam, Indonesia, Malaysia, Thailand
2009 – SOM II	Papua New Guinea, Philippines, Russia, Viet Nam

broaden the coverage of the IAP. The existing structure was felt to be too limiting to allow for the listing of voluntary actions arising from specific APEC initiatives (including the many Collective Action Plans — CAPs and the programmes emanating from the Working Groups).[6]

Most of the above comments were taken up by APEC in the efforts to improve its framework for the IAP peer review. Ministers agreed to review the IAP Peer Review Guidelines and to give attention to what member economies were doing individually and collectively to implement specific APEC commitments and priorities. They also agreed to launch the second three-year cycle of the peer review (2007–09) with a clear timetable for review of all 21 member economies.

Of significance was their effort to undertake the MSTS towards achieving the Bogor Goals. Although it was recognized that the trade and investment policy landscape has changed considerably, the Stock Taking concluded that the Bogor Goals remain as relevant as they were in 1994 (APEC 2005). It noted the increased importance of behind-the-border measures for APEC. The APEC Report on the Stock Taking also reiterated the strength of the APEC forum due to its flexibility as well as its consensus-based and non-binding decisions. This point appears to have been made in response to discussions about the need to review APEC's voluntary nature (Soesastro 2005).

However, the Stock Taking called on member economies to become more committed to implement APEC decisions, and that these decisions need to be supported by more effective, targeted and demand-driven capacity building. It was further argued that the agenda required to further drive growth in the region should be broadened from what was envisaged in 1994. Therefore, the IAP review process needs to address capacity-building strategies to assist individual economies in reaching APEC targets. The Busan Roadmap and the Busan Business Agenda were seen as a pragmatic manifestation of APEC's efforts to achieve its goals in a new environment (Elek 2005).

The Mid-Term Stock Taking did not provide an assessment of the IAPs and the performance of individual APEC member economies in implementing their commitments to achieving the Bogor Goals. It reiterated the earlier calls for increased transparency and accessibility to business. It highlighted that the IAP Peer Review process needed to be "made more robust, forward-looking and policy relevant interaction as well as to include a greater focus on what APEC members are doing individually and collectively to implement specific APEC commitments and priorities". The latter suggestion was meant to bring out APEC's value added.

Elsewhere it has been argued that "the real value added by APEC is the collective political will, leadership and commitment of 21 APEC leaders that could be put to bear on global, regional and bilateral negotiations for binding trade and investment liberalization agreements" (Romeo Reyes, *Jakarta Post*, 1 December 2005). This is indeed an important value added and is essentially a major rationale for APEC's creation.

This will lies beyond the scope of even a further enhanced IAP Peer Review process that by its nature focuses on actions by individual member economies. Although APEC value added is important, Yamazawa (2009) has argued that focusing the review on it is not sufficient.

The second three-year cycle of the enhanced peer review (2007–09) involves two independent experts in each Review Team because of the broadening of the scope of the review. For instance, it now includes consideration of the broader trade policy measures of member economies. One wonders, however, whether some of these assessments would simply duplicate efforts undertaken elsewhere, such as the Trade Policy Review Mechanism of the WTO.

Improving the Process: Issues for Consideration

The peer review process has moved in the direction of a broadening of its scope since the guidelines provided by the OAA in 1995 are thought to have become too restrictive. But some assessments focus on the need to make the format of the IAPs more specific with clear mid-term and long-term targets (Han 2005).

Various suggestions have been put on the table. One suggestion is to focus the IAP Review Process on sectors and not on economies (Chan 2005). Yamazawa (2009) thought that IAPs should not only report on the impediments that have and will be liberalized but also those that still remain in place.

A question that continues to haunt APEC is why it cannot come up with a clear definition of the Bogor Goals of "free and open trade and investment in the region". In the process of the Mid-Term Stock Taking there was hope that APEC would finally be able to provide a clear definition of the Bogor Goals. Instead, as reported by Chan (2005), it was also felt that pressing for a definition would spoil the intended (constructive) ambiguity.

It is remarkable that the official website of the Philippines Tariff Commission (http://tariffcommission.gov.ph/asia.html) made reference to a set of "operational targets set by the APEC leaders in Osaka to achieve the goal of free and open trade and investment in the Asia-Pacific region by 2020" that does not appear to have been agreed on. These targets included among others: (a) zero tariffs for all goods and the removal of all quantitative restrictions; (b) unlimited rights of establishment, national treatment or travel related to the provision of services for visits of up to two years; (c) national treatment of all firms and unrestricted rights of establishment in all sectors of production, including national treatment of international investors in terms of fiscal policy (taxation and/or subsidies); (d) full harmonization of air traffic control procedures and safety standards; (e) introduction of "smart card" passports and electronic processing of international passengers; (f) mutual recognition of all technical telecommunications standards, unhampered trans-border transmissions, and national treatment for connections to local telecommunications networks; and (g) adoption of an APEC Code of Practice for the settlement of disputes relating to trade policy or international investments based on mediation and the reinforcement of existing multilateral mechanisms.

It does appear that it no longer seems to be too difficult for all APEC members to agree on targets such as those listed above. However, as the 2010 date for the implementation of the Bogor Goals by developed member economies is nearing, it may be difficult for developed members to accept any set of targets on political grounds. This could be the reason why Yamazawa (2009) has introduced the notion of "graduation" in the process towards achieving the Bogor Goals. The developed members and certain developing members are placed in the "graduating group". They will be exempted from submitting annual IAPs, but they should set a post-Bogor agenda towards a higher level of liberalization. What Yamazawa has in mind is for this set of members to form their own free trade area. In his proposal, the remaining members will stay engaged with the Bogor commitments. It will be interesting to see the reactions to Yamazawa's radical suggestion. It is hard to imagine that APEC can agree to continuing with the IAP process that involves only a subset of its members.

The key issue is how to make the IAPs more meaningful. There will be a trade-off between maintaining a standard format and adjusting the format to APEC's plans and programmes. But whatever the case, the direction for the improvement has been clearly identified by ABAC that has been officially drawn into the peer review process. In a document on "ABAC Management of APEC IAP Review Process" prepared by ABAC Australia (APARWG27-006 dated 22 February 2007), ABAC concluded that the existing process is flawed: "In reality it is more of a 'rear view mirror' process since officials are reluctant to engage on future action and they are more content to talk about steps taken in the past. No one seems prepared to actually spell out what they need to do to reach (in their view) the Bogor Goals."

A peer review that is more forward looking will require a different process from the exiting one. What has been lacking is the overall strategic assessment of progress by the 21 members that could help identify what individual countries will need to do. The assessment by independent experts of the overall development should help transform the peer review meeting into a strategic forum. This may have to be undertaken at the Ministers rather than Senior Officials levels.

Notes

1. See for instance the joint paper by Yamazawa, Elek and Soesastro (1995).
2. The EPG formula entails the creation of a "temporary" or "partial" FTA.
3. In Thailand's observation, the EPG, being a creation of the APEC Ministers, should have reported their work through the SOM and Ministers and not directly to the APEC Leaders.
4. Based on personal communication at the Cebu SOM with the Indonesian SOM chair, Ambassador Soemadi Brotodiningrat.
5. Some crisis-affected member economies

made voluntary inclusions of financial sector reforms and other measures taken in response to the crisis in their IAPs.

6. The various initiatives launched by APEC Leaders should be added to the list.

References

APEC. *A Vision for APEC: Towards an Asia Pacific Economic Community*. Report of the Eminent Persons Group to APEC Ministers. Singapore: APEC Secretariat, October 1993.

———. *Achieving the APEC Vision: Free and Open Trade in the Asia-Pacific*. Second Report of the Eminent Persons Group. Singapore: APEC Secretariat, August 1994.

———. *Implementing the APEC Vision*. Third Report of the Eminent Persons Group. Singapore: APEC Secretariat, August 1995.

———. *A Mid-term Stocktake of Progress Towards the Bogor Goals — Busan Roadmap to Bogor Goals*, submitted to 17th APEC Ministerial Meeting by SOM Chair, Busan, Korea, 15–16 November 2005. Singapore: APEC Secretariat, 2005.

Bergsten, C. Fred. "Toward a Free Trade Area of the Asia Pacific". Remarks at the APEC CEO Summit, Santiago (Chile), 19 November 2004.

Chan, Mignonne M.J. "Don't Write Off APEC's Concerted Unilateralism Yet: A Reflection of Mid-Term Stocktaking". Paper presented at International Conference on "Building an Asia-Pacific Economic Community", 2005 APEC Study Center Consortium Conference and 2005 PECC Trade Forum, Hotel Shilla, Jeju, Korea, 15–22 May 2005.

Damond, Joseph. M. "The APEC Decision-Making Process for Trade Policy Issues: The Experience and Lessons of 1994–2001". In *APEC as an institution — Multilatertal governance in the Asia-Pacific*, edited by Richard E. Feinberg, pp. 85–110. Singapore: Institute of Southeast Asian Studies, 2003.

Elek, Andrew. "The Mid-term Review of the Bogor Goals: Strategic Issues and Options". In *The Future of APEC and Regionalism in Asia Pacific — Prespectives from the Second Track*, edited by Mark Borthwick et al., pp. 22–72. Jakarta: A joint publication of the Centre for Strategic and International Studies and the Pacific Economic Cooperation Council, 2005.

———. *APEC After Busan: New Direction*, KIEP APEC Study Series 05-01. Seoul: Korean Institute of International Economic Policy, 2005.

Han, Hognyul. "Achieving the Bogor Goal: the Bogor Action Plan". Paper presented at International Conference on "Building an Asia-Pacific Economic Community", 2005 APEC Study Center Consortium Conference and 2005 PECC Trade Forum, Hotel Shilla, Jeju, Korea, 15–22 May 2005.

Pacific Economic Cooperation Council (PECC). *Perspectives on the Manila Action Plan for APEC*. Manila, 1996.

———. *Assessing APEC Individual Action Plan and their Contribution to APEC's Goals*. Auckland, 1999.

Soesastro, Hadi. "Designing Mechanisms for Trade and Investment Liberalization in the Asia-Pacific". In *The New Asia-Pacific Order*, edited by Chan Heng Chee, pp. 220–45. Singapore: Institute of Southeast Asian Studies, 1997.

———. "APEC's Overall Goals and Objectives, Evolution and Current Status". In *APEC as an institution —*

Multilatertal governance in the Asia-Pacific, edited by Richard E. Feinberg, pp. 29–46. Singapore: Institute of Southeast Asian Studies, 2003.

———. "Re-writing APEC's Approach". In *The Future of APEC and Regionalism in Asia Pacific — Prespectives from the Second Track*, edited by Mark Borthwick et al., pp. 1–5. Jakarta: A joint publication of the Centre for Strategic and International Studies and the Pacific Economic Cooperation Council, 2005. Originally presented at the International Symposium on the Preparation for APEC 2005, Seoul (Korea), 11–13 July 2004.

Woo, Yuen Pau. "Review of the APEC Individual Action Plan Peer Review Process". In *The Future of APEC and Regionalism in Asia Pacific — Prespectives from the Second Track*, edited by Mark Borthwick et al., pp. 73–82. Jakarta: A joint publication of the Centre for Strategic and International Studies (Jakarta) and the Pacific Economic Cooperation Council, 2005. Originally presented at the APEC Study Centre Consortium Conference Organized by the Thai APEC Study Center, Thammasat University, Phuket, Thailand, 25–28 May 2003.

Yamazawa, Ippei. "APEC's Progress Toward the Bogor Target: A Quantitative Assessment of 1997 IAP/CAP". Tokyo: PECC Japan Committee (mimeo), 1998.

———. "How to Meet the Mid-term Bogor Goal?" draft paper, May 2009.

Yamazawa, Ippei with Andrew Elek and Hadi Soesastro. "Implementing the APEC Bogor Declaration: A Trade Liberalization Action Program". Paper presented at the PECC Trade Policy Forum VIII, Taipei, 20–21 April 1995.

Yamazawa, Ippei and Robert Scollay. "Towards an Assessment of APEC Trade Liberalization and Facilitation". In *APEC as an institution — Multilatertal governance in the Asia-Pacific*, edited by Richard E. Feinberg (ed.), pp. 111–30. Singapore: Institute of Southeast Asian Studies, 2003.

Yamazawa, Ippei and S. Urata. "Trade and Investment Liberalization and Facilitation". In *APEC: Challenges and Tasks for the Twenty-first Century*, edited by Ippei Yamazawa, pp. 57–97. Proceedings of the 25th Pacific Trade and Development Conference. London and New York: Routledge, 2000.

32. The APEC Secretariat Building in Singapore was officially opened on 6 September 2003.
Photo courtesy of the APEC Secretariat.

33. Bali, Indonesia was the host on 13 September 2005 for the Ocean Related Ministers representing 20 member economies. Their focus is to ensure that oceans and their resources provide a permanent and sustainable foundation to the economic and social well being of communities. This meeting continues from the Seoul Oceans Declaration that was adopted in 2002. *Photo courtesy of the APEC Secretariat.*

34. Concluding Senior Officials' Meeting held on 12 November 2005 at Busan, Korea under the host economy's theme "Towards One Community: Meet the Challenge and Make the Change". *Photo courtesy of the APEC Secretariat.*

35. Beautiful cultural costumes of the host economy are worn at the APEC Leaders' Meeting. Here APEC Leaders were photographed wearing the traditional Korean "durumagi" silk robes as they pose for an official photo in Busan, Korea, on 10 November 2005. *Photo courtesy of the APEC Secretariat.*

36. APEC Economic Leaders' Meeting, Sydney, Australia, September 2007. For the first time, a Declaration on Climate Change, Energy Security, and Clean Development was issued by APEC. *Photo courtesy of the APEC Secretariat.*

7

APEC at 20: Assessment of Trade/ Investment Liberalization, Facilitation and Ecotech Activities

Ippei Yamazawa

Ebbs and Flows in the Past Twenty Years

APEC will be celebrating its twentieth anniversary this year 2009. In 1989, it started as a series of meetings of Foreign and Trade Ministers from twelve member economies on economic cooperation in the Asia-Pacific region. Through the years, APEC has witnessed ebbs and flows in its momentum of cooperation.

Trade and investment liberalization and facilitation (TILF) has become one of APEC's major tasks since the first Economic Leaders Meeting in Seattle in 1993, where leaders jointly declared that they would "achieve free and open trade in Asia and Pacific". The Second Leaders meeting in Bogor, Indonesia, delivered the ambitious Bogor Declaration on "achieving liberalization by developed economies in 2010 and by the rest of economies in 2020". In 1995, the Osaka APEC adopted the Osaka Action Agenda (OAA) which provided concrete measures that can be taken to achieve the Bogor Goals.

The Committee for Trade and Investment (CTI) provided a common format in 1996 for Individual Action Plans (IAPs), in which individual member governments announced their own programmes to be implemented according to the OAA. CTI also produced a Collective Action Plan (CAP) regarding measures to be implemented collectively such as harmonized legislatures and systems. Thus IAPs included individual members' participation in CAP. The Manila APEC in November 1996 approved IAPs submitted by all member governments (Manila Action Plan for APEC, MAPA) and their implementation started in 1997.

The annual APEC gathering of Prime Ministers and Presidents of major economies with bold declarations often attracted the media's attention. Expectations for APEC became more heightened when participating members increased to 21 in 1998, covering all major economies surrounding the Pacific Ocean.

However, APEC encountered a big setback during the Asian financial crisis when several ASEAN members and the Republic of Korea (ROK) were severely hit, with their currencies depreciating substantially, and some suffering from negative growth rates. The EVSL (Early Voluntary Sector Liberalization), a breakthrough attempt of liberalization in the "easy sectors" also failed.[1] As such, the IAPs implemented since 1997 brought about much less liberalization than expected. Although it included the liberalization committed in the Uruguay Round Agreement (URA), its unilateral liberalization beyond the URA to be applied to other APEC members and non-members alike has been limited in terms of its coverage and depth. The URA liberalization was implemented on schedule as committed, but further liberalization in sensitive sectors has tended to be suspended. The Doha Development Agenda (DDA) negotiations which started in 2002 has also been protracted in recent years.

On the other hand, APEC itself has shifted to a more realistic line over the years. Its gravity has shifted from liberalization to trade facilitation, capacity building, and domestic reforms. The business environment has also changed in the Asia Pacific under an environment of accelerated globalization and prevailing regionalism of preferential trading arrangements. The Busan Roadmap was announced to include these realistic measures in 2005.

In November 2008, APEC responded in a timely manner to the expanding global economic crisis. In the G-20 Leaders Summit held on 15 November in Washington D.C., leaders decided to take urgent measures to stabilize financial markets and to carry out coordinated macroeconomic policies to restore growth and stability. In the following week, at the APEC Leaders Meeting which was held in Lima, Peru, the "Lima APEC Leaders' Statement on the Global Economy" (APEC 2008*a*, *b*) was issued. In the Statement, APEC Leaders strongly supported the Washington Declaration of the G-20 leaders and their Action Plan. APEC Leaders were committed to take broad policy responses needed to overcome the current crisis within 18 months and reiterated their firm belief that free market principles, and open trade and investment regimes should be the measures to continue to drive growth, employment and poverty reduction.

The G-20 Summit is expected to be the new framework underlying the management of the global economy. Through an expanded version of G-8, it is a collaborative framework on a global scale, involving major emerging economies like China, India, and Brazil plus mid-sized economies like Australia and South Korea. The G-20 needs to be supported by APEC and other major regional groups in order to ensure that the goals of the G-20 commitment are achieved. Nine member countries of APEC participated in G-20, thus providing a driving force for the framework. APEC has, however, not only been a framework for consensus building over policy coordination among members, but has also provided assistance to developing economy members by way of technology transfer and capacity building. In addition, there are issues of overlap. The G-20 will be tasked in future to address issues like environmental protection, disaster management, infectious disease prevention, anti-terrorism, poverty eradication and so on. These issues have already been addressed in the APEC framework. Nevertheless, APEC is expected to contribute by cooperating closely with G-20 to meet these challenges.

Bogor Goals as the Engine

APEC has pursued its liberalization and facilitation measures toward the Bogor Goals within the IAP/CAP framework. Its concrete design, the Osaka Action Agenda (OAA), had a comprehensive coverage of 14 areas of trade and investment liberalization and facilitation (see Table 7.1), and described measures to be implemented for each area. Facilitation measures aimed to reduce the cost of doing business by enhancing the transparency and certainty of rules, legislation and standards and harmonizing them between member economies, which are equally important to liberalization in order to enhance trade and investment in the region.

The IAP formula reflected APEC's unique modality of implementing liberalization and facilitation, that of "concerted unilateral liberalization" (CUL). Under this scheme, individual member economies unilaterally announced their own liberalization and facilitation programmes and implemented them in accordance with their domestic rules. However, individual member economies closely watched each other's liberalization programme and implementation and were obliged to submit liberalization programmes as broad-ranging as their neighbours and were encouraged to implement in line with their commitments. APEC relied upon peer pressure among members to urge all members to join in the liberalization efforts.

Individual APEC member governments have continued to revise their IAPs every year. The reporting has been made more elaborate and transparency improved in response to a common format. The number of liberalization measures increased as their Uruguay Round (UR) commitments were implemented. Voluntary liberalization was also added either in the form of accelerated implementation of the URA or reduction of applied tariffs from their UR rates in several member economies. The CAP helped individual members to introduce common practices such as the Summary Tables of Tariffs and NTMs. The CAP was especially effective in introducing new legislation of

TABLE 7.1
APEC's Three Activities

Liberalization
Osaka Action Agenda
Tariffs
Non-Tariff Measures
Services
Investment
Early Voluntary Sectoral Liberalization
Facilitation
Osaka Action Agenda
Standard and Conformance
Customs Procedures
Intellectual Property Rights
Government Procurement
Business Mobility
Deregulation
Competition Policy
Rules of Origin
Dispute Settlement
Implementation of the Uruguay Round Agreements
Economic and Technical Cooperation
Developing human capital
Developing stable and efficient markets through structural reform
Strengthening economic infrastructure
Facilitating technology flows and harassing technologies for the future
Safeguarding the quality of life through environmentaly sound growth
Developing and strengthening the dynamism of SMEs
Integration into the global economy
Human security and counter-terrorism
Promoting the development of knowledge-based economies
Addressing social dimension of globalization

facilitation consistent with the APEC system prescribed in the OAA. By and large, the IAP process encouraged individual member governments to implement liberalization and facilitation measures towards the Bogor Goals. One short-coming accompanying such implementation was its "positive list formula" in which the IAP reported only the impediments to be liberalized but not those still remaining. Thus the IAPs increased the volume but did not provide a comprehensive list of existing impediments.

In 2002–04 APEC's senior officials meeting (SOM) conducted a peer review process of individual members' IAPs so as to strengthen their efforts towards achieving the Bogor Goals. A team was formed on each member economy's IAP consisting of a senior official, one or two expert consultants, and an APEC Secretariat staff. Based on comments submitted by other members, the team interviewed government officials of the member economy under review and drafted a peer review report. The report was then submitted to a special session of the SOM chaired by the team's senior official, discussed in an open forum, and amended where necessary, thus encouraging the member under review to improve on its IAP implementation, closer towards the Bogor Goals.

Although individual teams followed a common format set by the SOM for the peer review report and reviewed each member's implementation by areas, the assessment stance differed between review teams. Many followed the WTO's Trade Policy Review Mechanism (TPRM) closely. The TPRM indicates departures from an economy's trade and investment policy from WTO rules and urges an economy to remove such gaps. Some reviewers have followed closely to the TPRM but they have tended to be more lenient towards developing economy members. APEC's IAP Peer Reviews should, however, differ from the TPRM. APEC's IAPs focus on an economy's liberalization and facilitation efforts reflecting its unique domestic conditions and does not request quick harmonization. Both the Bogor Goals and the OAA contain ambiguity and flexibility, some deliberate and some unintentional. Hence, it does not fit into APEC's modality to re-define rules strictly and to decide who passes and who fails, but to encourage as many members as possible to continue in their efforts to reach the Bogor Goals. This seems to be the fundamental objective of the IAP Peer Review.[2] In the meantime, SOM conducted the second round of peer review in 2007–09.

Liberalization

In this section, a review of the progress of liberalization by APEC member economies along the OAA (Table 7.1) will be presented.[3]

Tariffs: The OAA did not set the Bogor Goals at "zero tariffs for all commodities" but set it at simple average tariffs of between 0 and 5 per cent and to reduce high tariff items. Many APEC members have managed to reduce their tariffs due to the URA but high tariffs have remained in sensitive sectors under the protracted DDA negotiations. Most advanced economy members have reduced their simple average (applied) tariffs down to less than 5 per cent, with the exception of Japan and Canada whoes simple average tariffs have remained above 5 per cent due to high tariffs existing in agricultural products, textile and clothing. ASEAN members, Mexico and Peru have reduced their applied tariffs to below 10 per cent, while keeping the WTO bound tariffs to above 20–30 per cent. It can only be hoped that the Agricultural and Non-Agricultural Market Access negotiation be concluded in the DDA, so that remaining high peak tariffs in sensitive sectors and high bound tariffs can be reduced.

NTM: WTO admits Non-Tariff Measures (NTM) for reasons of health, public moral, and security, and many members have reported that they impose no NTMs inconsistent with WTO rules. The OAA listed six non-tariff measures: import quotas, surcharge, minimum import price, discretionary export/import licenses, voluntary export restriction, and export subsidies and instructed each economy to enhance the transparency of its respective laws, regulations and administrative procedures in relation to the flow of goods, services and capital among APEC economies and their gradual reduction. However, the NTM summary tables, requested by the Common Format, reported on the existence of NTMs in many sectors (except for New Zealand). It is hard to identify how many subsectors are subject to NTMs and how many of them are consistent with WTO. In the meantime, the import quota on agricultural products was tarifficated under the Uruguay Round Agriculture Agreement by 2000 and bilateral quota restriction on textiles and clothing items under Multi-fibre Agreement were abolished by 2005.

Services: The liberalization of services trade was only included in the Uruguay Round and much less has been achieved than that of commodity trade. Developing economy members have delayed in this area. Various regulations are imposed on services in domestic transactions and extended to cross-border transactions. The General Agreement on Trade in Services (GATS) was concluded in the Uruguay Round in which the standard sector classification for service trade was set and four modes of supply (cross-border supply, consumption abroad, commercial presence and presence of natural persons) and two aspects (national treatment and market access) were identified. Individual countries report on the existence of restriction for individual sector, mode, and aspect, and commit not to increase restrictions (GATS Commitment Table). However. even developed economy members keep restriction on many sectors, while developing economy members liberalize much fewer sectors.

Reflecting the delayed liberalization in services trade in the UR negotiations, the OAA set much less liberalization measures on services than on commodities. It only identified four sectors: telecommunications, transportation, energy, and tourism as priority sectors for liberalization. Individual members' IAPs express their intention of services liberalization and list sectors to be liberalized (positive list formula). It is hard to identify from the IAPs how many sectors still remain to be liberalized.

Some progress has been made in the services trade liberalization for the past 15 years. The service trade negotiation started in 2000 ahead of the DDA and two rounds of requests and offers were completed so that the chair's text was finalized at the ministerial meeting in July 2008. Its final conclusion has to wait the conclusion of Agriculture and Non-Agriculture Market Access negotiation, but some liberalization commitments have already been expressed in the IAPs.

WTO's database on services counts the number of sectors already liberalized (not bound in the commitment table) by individual members. Out of 55 sectors, developed economy members have liberalized about 30 sectors or more, while developing economy members commit liberalization in less than 30 sectors.

Investment: Each APEC member is eager to receive foreign investment for domestic development. As such, APEC adopted the Non-binding Investment Principles (NBIP) as a model measure for the investment environment in 1995. Many members report in their IAPs that their own foreign investment policies and legislation are consistent with the NBIP. Most economies have arranged investment laws and regimes and implemented protection and redemption of profits. Many economies have joined the WTO/TRIM agreement and set only minimum performance requirements, then restrict FDI or give incentives in only selected industries, and finally give national treatment to foreign investors. However, advanced developing economy members still keep FDI restrictions and incentives to protect strategic industries.

The World Bank's index for Ease of Doing Business gives an objective assessment of government rule-making on business activity for 181 countries. It includes laws and regulations for both domestic and foreign business and notes the high level of efficiency of APEC members. Eight APEC member economies are included in the top ten together with EU members and some oil producing countries, and 17 APEC members are ranked in the top half of the 181 countries.

Facilitation

In terms of the progress in facilitation areas according to the OAA (Table 7.1), the IAP/CAP framework worked better in these areas due to much less domestic resistance to facilitation.

Standard and Conformance (S&C): APEC issued "APEC's S&C Framework Declaration" in 1994 and established a Sub-Committee for S&C (SCSC) for joint efforts in alignment to international standards and mutual recognition of conformance assessment. Individual member's achievement, however, has been constrained. First, a member has to build its technical infrastructure for its own standards, then participate in the International Organization for Standardization (ISO), International Electro-technical Commission (IEC), and the Treaty of the Metre, etc. in order to align domestic to international standards, and start mutual recognition of conformance assessment with other partners. The TFAPII (2008) reported that 15 APEC members have adopted ISO, 16 members IEC, while 16 members participate in recognition of conformance in regulated sectors through the APEC Electrical and Electronic MRA, and Asia Pacific Laboratory Accreditation Cooperation multilateral MRAs.

Customs Procedures: The Sub-Committee on Custom Procedures (SCCP) has made great progress in modernizing customs administration in APEC member governments over the past years. This has included a substantial improvement in promptness, transparency and predictability in customs procedures, and an improved trade and investment environment for businesses across the region. Its impact is multiplied when it is implemented jointly by as many member governments as possible. The OAA set concrete objectives for collective action such as harmonization of tariff structure with the HS Convention, adoption of the principles of the WTO valuation agreement, simplification and harmonization on the basis of the Kyoto Convention, transparency of customs procedures, customs laws, regulations, administrative guidelines, procedures and rulings, and adoption of the UN/EDIFACT. Most members have adopted the first two objectives. The revised Kyoto Convention (RKC) has been in force since 2006 and all APEC members except Chinese Taipei have already adopted it. The UN/EDIFACT is implemented by many members and the average time length required for customs clearance has been significantly shortened.

Intellectual Property Rights (IPR): The protection of IPR is a prerequisite for technology and know-how to be transferred smoothly and better utilized across borders. The OAA set objectives to ensure the adequate and effective protection of IRP, including legislation, administration, and enforcement in the Asia-Pacific region based on the principles of MFN treatment, national treatment, transparency as set out in the WTO/TRIPs agreement (1994) and other related agreements. This has been well perceived by all APEC members and most members ratified TRIPs and Paris Convention for patents.

Government Procurement: With regard to government procurement, priority purchase of domestic products was long admitted because of national security and industry protection (exempted from national treatment in GATT Article 3). However, because of the globalization of businesses, government procurement transactions have necessitated a demand for an open and competitive market for government procurements. The Government Procurement Agreement (GPA) was ratified as a part of Marrakech Treaty in 1994, which covers both commodities and services and includes local governments and other public organizations as well. However, the decentralization of government administration differs among APEC members, and as such the OAA did not emphasize the liberalization of government procurement but insisted on the transparency of legislation and procedures and its international dissemination. In 1995 APEC adopted a model measure, Government Procurement Non-Binding Principles of Transparency, Value for Money, Open and Effective Competition, Fair Dealing, Accountability and Due Process, and Non-discrimination and encouraged individual members to align their own procedures to it. Half of APEC members have either ratified GPA or participated as observers.

Business Mobility: APEC economies have enhanced the mobility of business people engaged in trade and investment in the region. The focus is mainly on the processing of visas, the application procedures, and the terms of validity. APEC published the *APEC Business Travel Handbook* by collecting and disseminating information on such aspects. The APEC Business Advisory Council recommendation of the APEC Business Travel Card, and privileged lanes for guaranteed business travellers at the immigration office, has now been adopted by 21 APEC member economies. The time required for visa processing and the number of required documents have been reduced; multiple entry visas are issued by many members. Members have also strengthened anti-terrorism immigration procedures since 2001.

Economic and Technical Cooperation

The assessment in the preceding two sections still leaves five areas of the OAA — Deregulation, Competition Policy, Rules of Origin (ROO), Dispute Settlement, and Implementation of the URA (Table 7.1) — to be evaluated. As competition policy and deregulation have only been broadly stated in the OAA, and there is no consensus on the specific goals or scope of competition policy or deregulation among members (as they are at different stages of industrialization and operate under different institutional and legal structures), APEC members have not been able to report their IAPs in a standardized manner. These areas were considered "behind-the-border measures" and reset as the Structural Reform Program under Economic Committee in 2005.

The ROO originally aimed at collecting information about different ROOs in preferential and non-preferential ROOs among APEC members and promoting their harmonization. As the DDA negotiation has been protracted and unresolved, and bilateral and regional FTAs have been flourishing worldwide, ROOs have become Model Measures of FTAs. Dispute settlement is still an important task among APEC members. However, many members have tended to resort to the WTO panels for dispute settlement and the "APEC Dispute Mediation System" proposed by the EPG Report III has not been developed so far (APEC 1995). The implementation of the URA have been completed. Thus the first three areas are in the new APEC agenda but it is too early to assess their achievement.

APEC's third activities are in economic and technical cooperation for development. They had started after the first APEC ministerial meeting in 1989, ahead of liberalization and facilitation measures and restarted as Ecotech in Part II of the OAA (1995). Thirteen areas were identified, with numerous fora or task forces organized on individual cooperation issues under "lead shepherds". This reflects a typical APEC modality of managing projects on cooperation. A few member economies jointly propose a pet project and provide both expertise, funds, and other resources. Some member economies cooperate by participating in the project while other members do not object to the project unless it affects them adversely. APEC does not usually provide financial support because of a lack of central funding. Such projects in technical cooperation take the form of surveys, research, and seminars. Thus over two hundred small projects flourished in the 1990s in this manner (Yamazawa 1997).

This modality was successful in a sense of mobilizing quite a few participants (from outside governments) with expertise and eagerness on individual cooperation issues across the Asia Pacific. But they were criticized for being too numerous, based on too loose a management structure, with a lack of focus and visible achievements. Table 7.1, under Ecotech, cites ten current areas (APEC 2008*c*). Familiar areas like human capital, infrastructure, technology flow, and SMEs have remained but new issues have appeared like human security, quality of life, and responses to globalization. The same APEC modality has continued in the setting and management of its Ecotech activities.

Busan Roadmap

In 2005, the Korean host conducted a mid-term stock-taking of the IAPs in order to invigorate member economies' efforts in achieving the Bogor Goals. Member economies were asked to submit an assessment of their achievement by then (Mid-Term Stock-taking Report). The Korean Government's think-tank, the Korean Institute of Economic Policy (KIEP), formed an international expert team to examine the issue. Peer review reports and members' own assessment reports were analysed and the KIEP team presented a detailed comparison of individual members' achievement in each of 13 areas of the OAA (APEC 2005*b*, Attachment) and a summary of all APEC members' progress toward the Bogor Goals (APEC 2005*b*, Main Report). SOM produced a Mid-Term Stock-taking report and introduced a new action plan: the Busan Roadmap (APEC 2005*a*). The report was submitted to the ministerial meeting and the Leaders adopted the Busan Roadmap.

The Busan Roadmap emphasized changes in the business environment which includes specific reduction of business transaction costs in the Asia-Pacific region. APEC's gravity itself has shifted from liberalization to trade facilitation, capacity building, and domestic reform (beyond the border measures). The Busan Roadmap announced its rationale for these realistic measures rather than literally pursuing the Bogor Goals in the changed world.

The Busan Roadmap has been expanded further to include *Strengthening Regional Integration and Food Safety Cooperation* (Hanoi APEC 2006), *Structural Reform of Behind-the-Border Measures* (Sydney APEC 2007), *Trade Facilitation Action Plan II* and *APEC's Model Measures for FTAs* (Lima APEC 2008). A greater contribution of APEC is expected in the trade and investment area during the current global economic crisis.

APEC's Agenda for 2010

Japan, in hosting APEC in 2010, has a big task of graduating developed economy members from the Bogor commitment. Indeed, the liberalization task has remained incomplete in sensitive sectors under the current DDA round. For APEC, an alternative choice will be to suspend the mid-term Bogor Goals but encourage all members to pursue the enlarged version, the Busan Roadmap.[4]

A strategic choice lies between the two. Either will encourage APEC members to further enhance liberalization in parallel with the DDA. This is consistent with the task that APEC has to achieve in the process of recovering from the current world economic crisis. I would like to suggest the graduation route for the following reasons.

First, the momentum of APEC has decreased since the Asian crisis in 1997–98: APEC needs to be reactivated. As a matter of fact, the APEC Business Advisory Group (ABAC) proposed an FTA for Asia Pacific (FTAAP) in order to promote the APEC liberalization. ABAC commissioned PECC to undertake a supportive study. Incidentally, four APEC members (Brunei Darussalam, Chile, New Zealand, and Singapore) had already formed a high-level FTA (P4 Group) in 2006 and the office of the United States Trade Representative (USTR) had expressed interest in joining the P4 in 2008 (now transformed into the Trans-Pacific Partnership, TPP).

Second, APEC has overloaded itself with too many tasks related to liberlization, such as *Strengthening Regional Integration, Structural Reform, Model Measures for FTAs* and *TFAPII* as mentioned above. We need to acknowledge its achievements to date and renew its action plan.

Third, its IAP formula needs some streamlining. It has served as a main engine of encouraging individual members' unilateral efforts towards achieving the Bogor Goals as mentioned above, but the IAP reports have become huge documents with "positive lists" of liberalization and facilitation measures that are cumbersome and long.

Adopting the graduation route that literally follows the Bogor Declaration, the present author would like to suggest the APEC Agenda for 2010 to consist of the following three pillar tasks.

(A) Graduate "5 + α" member economies from the Bogor commitment, and exempt them from the IAP submission every year.

(B) Encourage the rest of the members to keep engaged in the Bogor commitment

(C) Set a post-Bogor agenda for the graduating group towards a higher level of liberalization, such as the FTAAP and TFP as well as the remaining agenda in the Busan Roadmap.

Under A, the "5" represent APEC's developed economy members and α includes Singapore, Chile and Hong Kong China which have already achieved a high level of liberalization. APEC has already adopted the path-finder approach in which some ready members may go ahead of others, so that the FTAAP and TFP can be incorporated as a long-term target. We also expect that not all members of the second group will remain in the group until 2020, but some will graduate half way and join the first group. So will some ASEAN members as its Economic Community agenda proceeds towards 2015.

Taking advantage of its capable membership and twenty years of experience, APEC should also tackle new global challenges such as the environment, energy issues, epidemics, widened gaps and social safety-nets. It should also focus on closer cooperation in macro-economic policies and financial stability.

Notes

1. The failure of EVSL resulted from its attempt at reducing tariffs and NTMs in the "not easy" sectors or sectors which had the highest resistance to liberalization, such as the forestry and fish products sector, in the WTO formula (Yamazawa and Urata 2000).
2. Woo (2005) criticized this tendency of the IAP peer review report to follow the TPRM while characterizing them as incomplete reports of the members' trade policies and insisted that it should identify APEC's value added in individual IAPs. The present author also served as a consultant and shared Woo's criticism of many of the review reports following the TPRM. However, it is too strict an assessment of individual members' approach towards the Bogor Goals to focus on just APEC's value added alone.
3. The present author conducted a quantitative assessment of APEC's liberalization and facilitation in 1997, which was based more on future commitments while the present assessment examined the current achievements (Yamazawa and Urata 2000).
4. Elek (2005) seems to suggest this alternative for APEC in his review of the Mid-term Stock-taking Report (APEC 2005*a* & *b*).

References

APEC. *Implementing the APEC Vision*, Third Report of the Eminent Persons Group, August 1995.

———. *A Mid-term Stocktake of Progress Towards the Bogor Goals — Busan Roadmap to Bogor Goals*, submitted to 17th APEC Ministerial Meeting by SOM Chair. Busan Korea, 15–16 November 2005*a*.

———. *Bogor Goals Mid-term Stocktake — Project Team Experts' Report* — with Attachment: Progress on specific trade and investment barriers, 2005*b*.

———. *Lima APEC Leaders Statement on the Global Economy*, 22 November 2008*a*.

———. *Additional Document Delivered by Leaders Raised Further Measures to Deal with Global Financial Crisis*. Lima, 23 November 2008*b*.

———. *Senior Officials' Report on Economic and Technical Cooperation*. Singapore, November 2008*c*.

Elek, Andrew. *APEC After Busan: New Direction*. KIEP APEC Study Series 05-01, KIEP, 2005.

Woo, Yuen Pao. "A Review of the APEC Individual Action Plan Peer Review Process". In *The Future of APEC and Regionalism in Asia Pacific: Perspectives from the Second Trade*, edited by PECC. CSIS Indonesia and PECC, 2005.

Yamazawa, Ippei. "APEC's Economic and Technical Cooperation: Evolution and Tasks Ahead". In *Whither APEC?: Progress to Date and Agenda for the Future*, edited by F. Bergsten. Institute for International Economics, Washington D.C., 1997.

Yamazawa, I. and S. Urata. "Trade and Investment Liberalization and Facilitation". Chapter 3 in *APEC: Challenges and Tasks for the Twenty-first Century*, Proceedings of the 25th Pacific Trade and Development Conference, Routledge, London and New York, 2000.

37. The APEC Ministers for Trade Retreat, on 1 June 2006 in Ho Chi Minh City, Viet Nam, discussed the importance of APEC's contribution to the WTO Development Agenda (DDA) negotiations, WTO capacity building for APEC member economies, and the importance of high quality, transparency and broad consistency in RTAs/FTAs in achieving the Bogor Goals of free and open trade and investment in the region. The theme of Viet Nam's APEC 2006 meeting was "Towards a Dynamic Community for Sustainable Development and Prosperity". *Photo courtesy of the APEC Secretariat.*

38. The theme of this APEC meeting was "Strengthening SME Competitiveness for Trade and Investment" aimed at identifying the best policies and entrepreneurial practices in the APEC region. The meeting was attended by APEC Ministers and their representatives responsible for SMEs (small and medium enterprises). Also in attendance were the Executive Director of the APEC Secretariat, the APEC Business Advisory Council and official observers. *Photo courtesy of the APEC Secretariat.*

39. The 19th APEC Ministerial Meeting was held in Sydney, Australia from 5 to 6 September 2007. Its main focus areas were promoting prosperity through a commitment to trade and economic reform, enhancing human security in the Asia Pacific, and ensuring APEC remains dynamic and responsive to developments in the Asia Pacific to ensure that the APEC community remained vibrant and relevant. *Photo courtesy of the APEC Secretariat.*

40. The SMEs Second ABAC Summit focused on SMEs sharing their successes with one another. This was held in November 2008 at the Real Felipe Fortress Convention Center in Callao, Peru. *Photo courtesy of the APEC Secretariat.*

41. APEC Economic Leaders' Meeting, Peru, Lima, November 2008. APEC Economic Leaders addressed the global financial crisis in the Lima Statement on the Global Economy. *Photo courtesy of the APEC Secretariat.*

8

Integrating the Business Community in the APEC Process: Genesis of the Pacific Business Forum

Tommy Koh
Lee Tsao Yuan
Arun Mahizhnan

Introduction

On a clear November day in 1993, some of the world's most powerful political leaders had a good idea to boost economic development: they decided to engage the people who are most directly involved in economic development — the business community.

Though APEC was inaugurated in 1989, it was not till 1993 that a schedule of annual meetings of the top leaders of APEC was set in place. The very first Leaders Meeting was held on the serene and beautiful Blake Island, near Seattle, in 1993, under the chairmanship of President Bill Clinton. At this meeting, the Leaders decided to ask the business community of APEC to establish a forum to "identify issues APEC should address to facilitate regional trade and investment and encourage the further development of business networks throughout the region". Thus was born the Pacific Business Forum (PBF), later renamed as the APEC Business Advisory Council (ABAC).

The PBF was perhaps the first ever formal and independent business forum that was to be appended to the annual summit of a major grouping of economies. In the past, though economic development was often at the top of the agenda in many international groupings, political leaders and government officials rarely engaged the business community directly and formally in their meetings. APEC Leaders made a significant departure from this practice and decided to integrate the business community as part of the APEC deliberative process. They personally appointed the PBF members and heard directly from them without the usual layers of intermediaries.

Establishment of PBF

The APEC Leaders' decision to establish the Pacific Business Forum was transmitted by a US emissary, Ms Sandra Kristoff, Assistant US Trade Representative, to Professor Tommy Koh who, while being an Ambassador-at-Large with the Government of Singapore, was also the head of a Singapore think-tank, the Institute of Policy Studies (IPS). Sandy Kristoff requested Koh to convene the first meeting of the PBF and for IPS to act as its Secretariat. The US probably felt that it was better for a small country than for the US to act as convenor. Singapore is small, friendly and acceptable to all the APEC members. Koh accepted the US request.

In convening the first meeting of the PBF, Koh and his working group proposed a framework for this Forum — the membership, the modus operandi for the meetings and the process of making final recommendations to the Leaders. The membership of PBF was, in some ways, preordained — it would have representation from each member economy of APEC and each representative would be personally nominated by the Leaders. It was also decided that in the first instance each economy would be invited to send two representatives, one representing large business and the other from the small and medium business sector. In the end, however, three economies preferred to send only one representative, thus making the total membership 33, instead of 36, in the first PBF.

The first PBF meeting was convened in Singapore in June 1994, and the group decided to elect two co-chairs for the Forum. The co-chairs were Mr Les McCraw, representing the current chairman and Mr Bustanil Arifin of Indonesia, representing the next chairman of APEC. In future, PBF would have a troika of co-chairs, representing the current chairman, the next chairman and the immediate past chairman.

The co-chairs and the PBF Secretariat were supported by a number of staffers drawn from the co-chairs' own companies and the APEC Secretariat, thus providing both professional and expert support for the Forum's deliberations. The IPS team, led by Tommy Koh, Lee Tsao Yuan and Arun Mahizhnan, the co-chairs' staffers and the APEC Secretariat officials worked harmoniously. We made several good friends with whom we have stayed in touch over the years.

Within a span of five months, the PBF met three times in Singapore: (a) 10–15 June; (b) 5–6 August; and (c) 2–3 September, and held extensive and spirited discussions on many written and oral submissions on what the PBF should focus on. From the level of small businesses to the level of global conglomerates, from passport control for frequent business travellers to international policy on trade and investment, from individual action to regional collaboration, every critical aspect affecting the business community's performance in regional economic development was put on the table. Despite initial apprehensions of potential conflict and divergence, the PBF managed to surprise many by submitting a comprehensive and consensual report to the APEC Leaders in October 1994, in Indonesia.

First PBF Report

The report was called "A Business Blueprint for APEC: Strategies for Growth and Common Prosperity". In the report, the PBF members first reiterated their independent stand in arriving at their conclusions, which might or might not coincide with their own government's views. Second, they pointed out that despite the very diverse levels of economic development in their different economies, they all shared the same business philosophy — "of doing business better, faster and more effectively" — which led to a prompt and prudent consensus on what needs to be done. Third, they set out their own vision for an Asia-Pacific region where dynamic and lasting growth will benefit all the peoples of the region and enhance the standard of living of all of them. They clearly signalled their preference for growth with equity over growth as the only objective. Finally, they offered a set of recommendations that would help fulfil that vision.

PBF Recommendations

Of all the recommendations of PBF's first blueprint for business growth, free trade and investment liberalization were considered to be the cornerstone of their strategies and programmes. It argued that without liberating the flow of goods, services, capital and labour within the region, all else would be captive to unproductive and self-serving regulations and barriers. Therefore, it recommended an immediate standstill on such new regulations and barriers and an accelerated dismantling of old ones. It even suggested a firm deadline for the liberalization of trade and investment throughout the APEC economies by 2010. In sum, this set of recommendations reflected the frustrations and impatience of a business community that was raring to grow beyond their national borders.

The blueprint also addressed other critical issues faced by the business community. Business facilitation was such an issue. The cumbersome variety of regulations and controls within the region, which rose from distant and different historical trends, further complicated by corruption and inefficiency, seriously inhibited businesses from crossing borders and growing fast. So the PBF made specific recommendations on simplifying and standardizing customs and immigrations rules and regulations, using new technology to speed up documentation processing as well as on training relevant officials with the knowledge and skill to implement the recommendations. The report also argued for improvements in intellectual property rights, setting up of mutual recognition agreements, the easing of restrictions on technology transfers and the establishment of dispute settlement mechanisms.

Another major concern for the business community centred on human resource development policies. The disparity in development of human resources across the region and the potential for great improvements in their capacity and skill sets prompted PBF to urge the Leaders to intensify region-wide training programmes as well as skills and technology transfer across borders. The report also pointed out that business development within the region could be speeded up with conducive policies that favoured small and medium enterprises, improved access to capital and offered substantial tax incentives. Businesses also needed rapid and well coordinated infrastructure development to facilitate economic development. To this end, the reported recommended the setting up of a joint public and business sector task-force on region-wide infrastructure development.

The report also stressed that the partnership between the government and the private sector should extend beyond infrastructure development into many other areas of mutual concern and benefit. In order to examine these areas of partnership as well as to dialogue with each other on a continual basis, the PBF recommended that the Leaders establish an APEC Business Advisory Forum which would report directly to them to help achieve APEC's long term objectives.

The above is not an exhaustive account either of the PBF process or the policy recommendations but only an indicative summary that would suggest the depth and breadth of the business community's concerns over regional economic development.

The first report of PBF was submitted to then APEC Chairman, President Soeharto of Indonesia, on 15 October 1994, for consideration by APEC leaders at their Bogor meeting in November that year.

PBF II

At their Bogor meeting, the Leaders adopted the goal of free and open trade and investment for all APEC economies by 2010 for developed economies and 2020 for developing economies in accordance with the recommendation of the APEC Group of Eminent Persons (EPG). The positive experience and outcome of the first round of PBF encouraged the Leaders to request PBF to continue its work. The Forum was asked to assess the progress of APEC, to provide further recommendations for increasing cooperation, and to review the interrelationships between APEC and the various subregional economic arrangements. However, subsequent to this request, an Eminent Persons Group took up the last area for further examination, leaving the PBF to focus on the first two aspects. The tone and temperament of the new brief was to move from a visioning exercise to an action mode. The second PBF did just that.

Through 1995, the PBF held three rounds of consultations among its members in order to prepare its second report to the Leaders' meeting in Osaka later that year. The three meetings were held in: (a) Singapore, 26–27 May;

(b) Tokyo, 14–15 July; and (c) Newport Beach, 1–2 September. The leadership of PBF now included a Japanese co-chair, Mr Minoru Morofushi, in addition to the two past co-chairs. As the first PBF report had provided a blueprint for business growth, the second report focused on specific action plans. Hence its title: "The Osaka Action Plan: Roadmap to Realising the APEC Vision".

PBF II Recommendations

The second PBF report was both shorter and sharper than the first, reflecting the concerns of both the Leaders and the business community to show some real action to overcome the "talk-shop" image APEC was acquiring after six years of existence. It made 15 specific recommendations in three broad areas: (a) a roadmap to 2020 with three components — guiding principles, agreement on timelines, and regular progress reviews; (b) 10 Osaka deliverables; and (c) two recommendations for business participation in APEC.

For reasons of brevity, the following is just a selection of those recommendations, to offer a sense of the concerns and the urgency the region's business community was feeling at that time.

In terms of guiding principles, the report cautioned that in creating an APEC-wide free trade and investment regime, there must be consistency with WTO rules. It also prudently argued for flexible consensus among member economies so that those lagging behind could catch up later. Given the overarching globalization process, the Forum also wanted to ensure that any regional agreement left room for inclusion of others by adopting the "open regionalism" concept. Perhaps the most problematic principle to implement, yet the most urgent would be PBF's call for transparency.

As timelines are an integral part of any action plan, the PBF report argued strongly for clear and agreed timelines for member economies to follow through. It also stressed the need for intermediate milestones so improvements could be measured and good examples could be shared among members to encourage those behind their targets. Above all, PBF urged that progress must be consistently and regularly reviewed, at various levels, including the Leaders level, so that the parties involved would feel the pressure to deliver on commitments.

In terms of deliverables, the report urged the Leaders to take a tactical as well as strategic approach. It argued that in addition to the final deadlines to be met in 2020, the Leaders should begin the process of implementation immediately, in Osaka. For example, PBF wanted the Leaders to announce in Osaka its intention to strengthen the APEC Non-Binding Investment Principles by the 1996 meeting in the Philippines. It wanted visa-free business travel throughout the region by 1999 and the first phase of it to be introduced in 1996. The report also addressed similar deliverables in areas such as customs harmonization, intellectual property rights, infrastructure development and human resource development.

In its recommendations on strengthening business community's participation in the APEC process, the most significant was, perhaps, the "self-destruct" proposal to establish the APEC Business Advisory Council (ABAC) which would automatically lead to the demise of PBF itself. The PBF was originally set up more as an exploratory consultative mechanism, without a long-term commitment to its continuation. The work of PBF over the two years had convinced the business community and those beyond in government and academia that a permanent advisory forum was needed to provide good counsel and strong support for the Leaders' various initiatives on the economic development of the region. Thus, PBF recommended that the Leaders announce the establishment of ABAC as its permanent advisory body at their Osaka meeting. The report also recommended regular and continuous involvement of business representatives in APEC's working groups to help formulate sound business policies and to help implement them effectively.

The second PBF report and recommendations were submitted to the Chairman of APEC, Prime Minister Maruyama of Japan, on 22 September 1995 in Tokyo, ahead of their Osaka meeting in November that year.

The PBF Experience

The notion of APEC leaders personally appointing business leaders from each of their economies to form a forum for business policy discussions and hearing directly from them without the intervention of any intermediaries was both unusual and untested when PBF was first mooted in 1993. Fortunately, for both the business community and the political leaders, the actual experience of the interactive process over the first two years turned out to be positive.

The business community of the Asia-Pacific region found, for the first time in their history, a common forum for them to critically but collegially address their serious business concerns, with the authority and influence bestowed on them by their respective Leaders. They also found, again for the first time, a direct channel to talk back to their Leaders.

The Leaders of APEC, for their part, made an unprecedented and potentially risky decision to engage the business leadership directly but, in the end, were rewarded by a frank, robust, thoughtful and constructive — though sometimes outspoken and critical — feedback on how to get things right and how to make things better. It seemed worth the risk.

Though the recommendations of PBF I & II were received with genuine interest on the part of the Leaders, its two-year life span was too short a time to determine the effectiveness of those recommendations. It is the case that even among those recommendations accepted by the Leaders, most needed long-term gestation and implementation to see the end results. It is also a fact that some of the short-term recommendations that were accepted were not actually implemented or effectively executed. However, some recommendations were accepted and swiftly implemented. One of them has resulted in hassle-free travel for our business people, travelling from one APEC economy to another in some but not all the member economies. At some airports, there are even designated lanes for APEC business travellers. The PBF scorecard was and had to be a work in progress. The entire region is watching that scorecard today, 15 years after its inception. In other chapters in this book, the reader will find some of those results.

Rebirth of PBF

The APEC Leaders accepted the recommendation to set up the new permanent advisor body, and PBF was re-born as ABAC at Osaka in November 1995. Koh and IPS relinquished their roles as PBF convenor and secretariat and handed over the responsibilities to Filipino colleagues, led by Mr Roberto Romulo, who set up the permanent international secretariat of ABAC in Manila. It is one of those reincarnations where good karma seems to lead to good consequences.

References

Report of the Pacific Business Forum. *A Business Blueprint for APEC: Strategies for Growth and Common Prosperity*. Singapore: APEC, 1994.

Report of the Pacific Business Forum. *The Osaka Action Plan: Roadmap to Realizing the APEC Vision*. Singapore: APEC, 1995.

42. At the Senior Officials' Meeting held between 12 and 23 August 2008 in Lima, Peru, APEC Senior Officials strongly supported the ongoing efforts in the WTO to reach a modalities agreement. *Photo courtesy of the APEC Secretariat.*

43. Arrival of the Malaysian Prime Minister and Finance Minister, Datuk Seri Najib Razak (second from left), at Lima, Peru, for the 16th APEC Economic Leaders' Meeting in November 2008. The theme for the 2008 Meeting was "A New Commitment to Asia-Pacific Development". *Photo courtesy of the APEC Secretariat.*

44. APEC Senior Officials meeting in February 2009 in Singapore reaffirmed their commitment to resist protectionist pressures, and agreed on initiatives to accelerate regional economic integration. The APEC Focus for 2009 Singapore APEC Year is "Sustaining Growth, Connecting the Region" which builds on APEC's work to date in promoting growth, cooperation, trade and investment across the APEC region. *Photo courtesy of the APEC Secretariat.*

Appendices

Appendix 1
APEC Member Economies: General Economic Indicators

Member Economy and Year Joined	*Land area ('000 sq km)*	*Population (millions)*		*GDP in PPP valuation (bil international dollars)*		*GDP per capita (international dollars)*		*GDP Rank (PPP valuation; out of 181 countries)*	
		Year joined	*2008*	*Year joined*	*2008*	*Year joined*	*2008*	*GDP*	*GDP per capita*
Australia (1989)	7,692	16.85	21.32	284.05	795.31	16,861	37,299	18	16
Brunei Darussalam (1989)	6	0.25	0.39	8.74	19.68[a]	35,520	50,117[a]	119	5
Canada (1989)	9,971	27.22	33.26	520.97	1,303.23	19,140	39,183	14	14
Chile (1994)	757	13.99	16.75	95.50	243.04	6,824	14,510	44	57
China, People's Rep of (1991)	9,561	1,158.23	1,327.66	1,028.09	7,916.43	888	5,963	2	101
Hong Kong, China (1991)	1	5.82	7.01	106.78	307.07	18,362	43,811	39	7
Indonesia (1989)	1,905	179.14	227.83	248.28	908.24	1,386	3,987[a]	16	122
Japan (1989)	378	123.03	27.69	2,113.94	4,354.37	17,183	34,100[a]	3	25
Korea, Republic of (1989)	99	42.45	48.55	308.53	1,342.34	7,268	27,647[a]	13	33
Malaysia (1989)	330	17.35	27.30	77.35	384.12	4,458	14,072	30	61
Mexico (1993)	1,958	87.95	106.32	721.45	1,548.01[a]	8,203	14,560[a]	11	55
New Zealand (1989)	271	3.37	4.28	44.27	115.71	13,133	27,060[a]	61	35
Papua New Guinea (1993)	463	4.29	6.20	7.12	13.04	1,661	2,105[a]	132	142
Peru (1998)	1,285	24.45	28.66	118.32	245.88	4,840	8,580[a]	43	84
Philippines (1989)	300	60.10	90.35	100.59	320.38[a]	1,674	3,546[a]	36	124
Russian Federation (1998)	17,098	147.80	142.00	923.61	2,260.91	6,249	15,922[a]	6	53
Singapore (1989)	1	2.93	4.67	45.76	238.76	15,612	51,142[a]	46	4
Chinese Taipei (1991)	36	20.61	23.04	217.07	711.42[a]	10,535	30,881[a]	19	26
Thailand (1989)	513	55.29	66.40	141.17	546.10	2,553	8,225	24	87
United States (1989)	9,364	247.29	304.42	5,484.35	14,264.60	22,178	46,859[a]	1	6
Viet Nam (1998)	332	75.46	86.35[a]	95.05	240.36	1,260	2,784[a]	45	129
Total APEC			2,700.42		38,078.99				
World total			6,653.43		68,996.85				
APEC's % share in world total			40.6		55.2				

Note: [a] Preliminary estimates.

Source: International Monetary Fund, World Economic Outlook Database, April 2009.

Appendix 2
Merchandise Trade in APEC, 1989

	Exports		*Exports to APEC*			*Imports*		*Imports from APEC*		
	In mil USD	*% Share of world total*	*In mil USD*	*% Share of total exports*	*% Share of world total*	*In mil USD*	*% Share of world total*	*In mil USD*	*% Share of total imports*	*% Share of world total*
Australia	37,382	1.3	21,532	58	2.2	45,036	1.4	26,206	58	2.6
Brunei Darussalam	1,882	0.1	1,807	96	0.2	859	0.03	628	73	0.06
Canada	120,681	4.0	96,313	80	10.0	129,095	4.1	95,443	74	9.3
Indonesia	21,944	0.7	16,581	76	1.7	16,470	0.5	9,653	59	0.9
Japan	274,788	9.2	152,191	55	15.7	209,646	6.7	108,625	52	10.6
Korea, Republic of	60,558	2.0	40,206	66	4.2	60,210	1.9	40,862	68	4.0
Malaysia	25,052	0.8	17,142	68	1.8	22,592	0.7	15,283	68	1.5
New Zealand	8,899	0.3	5,316	60	0.5	8,816	0.3	5,535	63	0.5
Philippines	7,755	0.3	5,470	71	0.6	11,171	0.4	6,545	59	0.6
Singapore	44,808	1.5	26,691	60	2.8	49,697	1.6	29,954	60	2.9
Thailand	20,190	0.7	11,099	55	1.1	25,378	0.8	15,334	60	1.5
United States	363,938	12.2	161,838	44	16.7	493,387	15.9	238,742	48	23.3
Total APEC	987,877	33.1	556,186	56	57.5	1,072,356	34.5	592,810	55	57.9
Other countries	1,999,563	66.9	411,635	21	42.5	2,038,794	65.5	430,521	21	42.1
Total world	2,987,440	100.0	967,821	32	100.0	3,111,150	100.0	1,023,332	33	100.0

Source of basic data: International Monetary Fund, Direction of Trade Statistics.

Appendix 3
Merchandise Trade in APEC, 2008

	Exports		Exports to APEC			Imports		Imports from APEC		
	In mil USD	*% Share of world total*	*In mil USD*	*% Share of total exports*	*% Share of world total*	*In mil USD*	*% Share of world total*	*In mil USD*	*% Share of total imports*	*% Share of world total*
Australia	185,693	1.2	136,683	74	2.0	211,111	1.3	146,873	70	2.0
Brunei Darussalam[1]	9,487	0.1	9,406	99	0.1	2,654	0.02	2,267	85	0.03
Canada	456,485	2.9	396,907	87	5.7	449,077	2.7	340,804	76	4.6
Chile[1]	71,348	0.4	39,882	56	0.6	55,960	0.3	29,259	52	0.4
China, People's Rep of[1]	1,468,830	9.2	906,921	62	13.0	1,215,310	7.3	691,877	57	9.3
Hong Kong, China	362,985	2.3	280,413	77	4.0	388,947	2.3	340,575	88	4.6
Indonesia	137,022	0.9	103,739	76	1.5	129,274	0.8	100,421	78	1.4
Japan	783,149	4.9	574,419	73	8.2	761,803	4.6	468,128	61	6.3
Korea, Republic of[1]	417,274	2.6	286,614	69	4.1	433,311	2.6	282,775	65	3.8
Malaysia[1]	219,790	1.4	171,479	78	2.5	185,573	1.1	145,782	79	2.0
Mexico[1]	271,137	1.7	228,798	84	3.3	302,910	1.8	240,671	79	3.2
New Zealand	30,618	0.2	21,001	69	0.3	34,203	0.2	24,875	73	0.3
Papua New Guinea[1]	8,811	0.1	4,463	51	0.1	3,394	0.02	3,176	94	0.04
Peru[1]	29,628	0.2	18,236	62	0.3	27,739	0.2	15,586	56	0.2
Philippines[1]	64,905	0.4	55,365	85	0.8	77,588	0.5	61,193	79	0.8
Russian Federation[1]	464,140	2.9	66,974	14	1.0	275,960	1.6	87,113	32	1.2
Singapore	339,414	2.1	251,306	74	3.6	319,779	1.9	214,341	67	2.9
Chinese Taipei	243,799	1.5	193,766	79	2.8	239,449	1.4	160,237	67	2.2
Thailand	173,235	1.1	118,092	68	1.7	178,526	1.1	114,759	64	1.5
United States	1,300,190	8.1	753,740	58	10.8	2,166,020	12.9	1,313,222	61	17.7
Viet Nam[1]	60,268	0.4	41,595	69	0.6	82,488	0.5	69,200	84	0.9
		0.0								
Total APEC	7,098,208	44.3	4,659,800	66	66.6	7,541,076	45.1	4,853,135	64	65.4
Other countries	8,911,692	55.7	2,333,217	26	33.4	9,196,724	54.9	2,565,531	28	34.6
Total world	16,009,900	100.0	6,993,016	44	100.0	16,737,800	100.0	7,418,666	44	100.0

Note: [1] Preliminary estimates.
Sources of basic data: International Monetary Fund, Direction of Trade Statistics; Chinese Taipei, Bureau of Foreign Trade website (http://eweb.trade.gov.tw; accessed on 25 August 2009).

Appendix 4
Regional Trade Agreements (RTAs) in Force among APEC Member Economies

RTA Name	*Coverage*	*Type*	*Date of entry into force*
ASEAN – China (G)	Goods	PTA	1-Jul-03
ASEAN – China (S)	Services	EIA	1-Jul-07
ASEAN Free Trade Area (AFTA)	Goods	FTA	28-Jan-92
Asia Pacific Trade Agreement (APTA)[1]	Goods	PTA	1-Jan-02
Australia – Chile	Goods & Services	FTA & EIA	6-Mar-09
Australia – New Zealand (ANZCERTA) (G)	Goods	FTA	1-Jan-83
Australia – New Zealand (ANZCERTA) (S)	Services	EIA	1-Jan-89
Australia – Papua New Guinea (PATCRA)	Goods	FTA	1-Feb-77
Brunei Darussalam – Japan	Goods & Services	FTA & EIA	31-Jul-08
Canada – Chile	Goods & Services	FTA & EIA	5-Jul-97
Canada – Peru	Goods & Services	FTA & EIA	1-Aug-09
Chile – China	Goods	FTA	1-Oct-06
Chile – Japan	Goods & Services	FTA & EIA	3-Sep-07
Chile – Mexico	Goods & Services	FTA & EIA	1-Aug-99
China – Hong Kong, China	Goods & Services	FTA & EIA	1-Jan-04
China – New Zealand	Goods & Services	FTA & EIA	1-Oct-08
China – Singapore	Goods & Services	FTA & EIA	1-Jan-09
Japan – Indonesia	Goods & Services	FTA & EIA	1-Jul-08
Japan – Malaysia	Goods & Services	FTA & EIA	13-Jul-06
Japan – Mexico	Goods & Services	FTA & EIA	1-Apr-05
Japan – Philippines	Goods & Services	FTA & EIA	11-Dec-08
Japan – Singapore	Goods & Services	FTA & EIA	30-Nov-02
Japan – Thailand	Goods & Services	FTA & EIA	1-Nov-07
Korea, Republic of – Chile	Goods & Services	FTA & EIA	1-Apr-04
Korea, Republic of – Singapore	Goods & Services	FTA & EIA	2-Mar-06
Latin American Integration Association (LAIA)[2]	Goods	PTA	18-Mar-81
New Zealand – Singapore	Goods & Services	FTA & EIA	1-Jan-01
North American Free Trade Agreement (NAFTA)[3]	Goods & Services	FTA & EIA	1-Jan-94
Peru – Singapore	Goods & Services	FTA & EIA	1-Aug-09
Singapore – Australia	Goods & Services	FTA & EIA	28-Jul-03
Thailand – Australia	Goods & Services	FTA & EIA	1-Jan-05
Thailand – New Zealand	Goods & Services	FTA & EIA	1-Jul-05
Trans-Pacific Strategic Economic Partnership[4]	Goods & Services	FTA & EIA	28-May-06
US – Australia	Goods & Services	FTA & EIA	1-Jan-05
US – Chile	Goods & Services	FTA & EIA	1-Jan-04
US – Peru	Goods & Services	FTA & EIA	1-Feb-09
US – Singapore	Goods & Services	FTA & EIA	1-Jan-04

Notes: PTA –- Preferential Trade Agreement; EIA – Economic Integration Agreement;
FTA – Free Trade Agreement.

[1] Accession of China to original 1976 agreement. APEC member economy signatories: Republic of Korea and China.

[2] APEC member economy signatories: Chile, Mexico, and Peru.

[3] Signatories: Canada, Mexico, and United States.

[4] Signatories: Brunei Darussalam, Chile, New Zealand, and Singapore.

Source: World Trade Organization, Regional Trade Agreements Database (http://rtais.wto.org; accessed on 31 August 2009).

Appendix 5
Regional Trade Agreements (RTAs) among APEC Member Economies for which an Early Announcement has been made to the WTO

RTA Name	*Launch of negotiations*
Australia – China	23-May-05
Australia – Malaysia	19-May-05
Canada – Colombia – Peru	7-Jun-07
Canada – Singapore	21-Oct-01
Japan – ASEAN	Early entry into force – signed on 14-Apr-2008
Japan – Australia	1-Apr-07
Japan – Korea, Republic of	1-Dec-03
Japan – Viet Nam	1-Jan-07
Korea, Republic of – ASEAN	30-Nov-04
Korea, Republic of – Canada	15-Jul-05
Korea, Republic of – Mexico	7-Feb-06
Korea, Republic of – US	Early announcement – signed on 30-Jul-07

Source: World Trade Organization, Regional Trade Agreements Database (http://rtais.wto.org; accessed on 31 August 2009).

Index

B

U

V

Y

Z

APEC Member Economies

Australia
Brunei Darussalam
Canada
Chile
People's Republic of China
Hong Kong, China
Indonesia
Japan
Republic of Korea
Malaysia
Mexico
New Zealand
Papua New Guinea
Peru
Philippines
Russia
Singapore
Chinese Taipei
Thailand
United States
Viet Nam

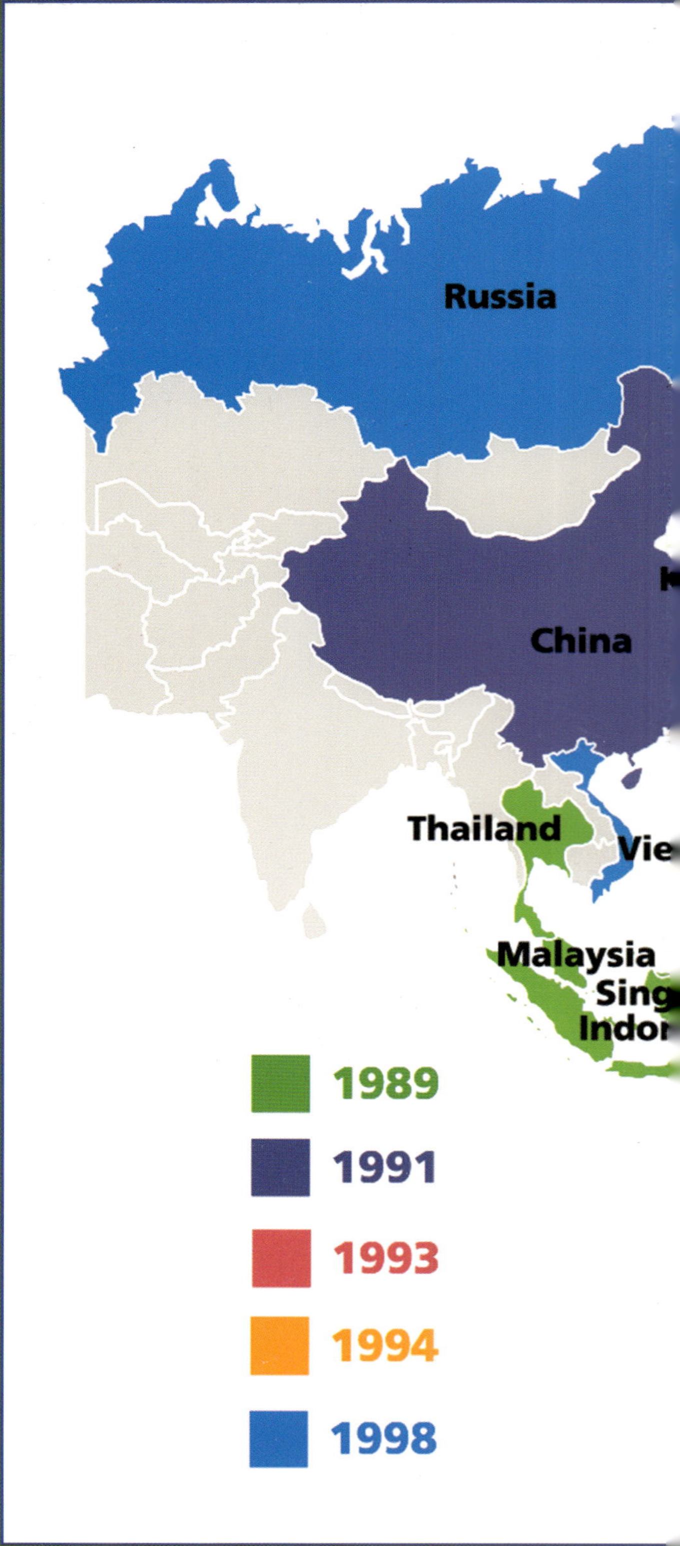